THE WAY OF THE ORISA

//////////

THE WAY OF THE ORISA

EMPOWERING YOUR LIFE
THROUGH THE ANCIENT AFRICAN
RELIGION OF IFA

PHILIP JOHN NEIMARK

FAGBAMILA
OLUWO OF IFA

HarperOne
An Imprint of HarperCollinsPublishers

HarperOne

All photographs are used courtesy of Justine Cordwell.

HarperCollins books may be purchased for educational, business, or sales promotional use. For information, please e-mail the Special Markets Department at SPsales@harpercollins.com.

HarperCollins Web site: http://www.harpercollins.com

HarperCollins®, 🏭®, and HarperOne™ are trademarks of HarperCollins Publishers.

Library of Congress Cataloging-in-Publication Data

Neimark, Philip John.
  The way of Orisa: empowering your life through the
  ancient African religion of Ifa / Philip John Neimark (Fagbamila,
  Oluwo of Ifa). — 1st ed.
     p. cm.
  Includes index.
  ISBN: 978–0–06–250557–6
  1. Ifa. I. Title.
BF1779.I4N45. 1993
299'.68333—dc20   92–53903

23 24 25 26 27 LBC 37 36 35 34 33

To Vassa, whose love and faith pulled me along the path
To Tanya, Joshua, and Dashiel, who assure my return
To Afolabi Epega, who accepted and taught
To Caroline Pincus, who understood and made it understandable
To Orunmila Youngsters International, who rekindle the flame
. . . and to my father, Mortimer, and my mother, Hortense, whose
    blood flows through my veins

In addition I would like to acknowledge FAMA (F.A.M. Adewale-
Somadhi), whose source work on the Essence of Sacrifice and
other areas contributed greatly to this work; Chief Okemuyiwa
Akinyomilo (Akirabata-Ribiti), who provided the translation of
the Holy Works of Okanrun-Ofun for the Sacred Garden section;
Gbolahan Okemuyiwa and Awo Ademola Fabunmi, whose work
and translations on the concept of Ori proved invaluable; and a
host of other dedicated priests and priestesses whose knowledge,
insights, and wisdom contributed to this manuscript.

CONTENTS

The search for answers to the questions, Why are we here? and What mysterious forces created us . . . and sometimes seem to turn against us? has become part of the lifeways and accumulated knowledge of human beings all over the world. Perhaps older than speech, these thoughts coalesced into mythology when language evolved. The mythologies of peoples the world over attempted not only to answer these questions but to lay down the general "truths" of the creation of the earth and the specific natural forces involved and, in a very human way, to anthropomorphize these forces, to make them into understandable human forms with human traits.

Many types of religion evolved in Africa, nurtured by the wise men and women of that continent. Some of these institutionalized beliefs were simple and uncomplicated, developed by hunters and gatherers who were concerned only peripherally with a far-off creator god but intimately involved with a few immediate deities who controlled the winds and rains and brought game and a well-gathered harvest . . . or withheld them through natural disasters. In some African societies, like that of the Yoruba, people became sedentary horticulturists, developing a trade surplus and classes of specialists such as weavers, potters, blacksmiths, or metal casters. Out of economic surplus grew a hierarchical society, whose pattern was reflected in the complex religion of Ifa and the pantheon of gods of heaven and earth that Ifa brought into being. Over hundreds of years of development the Yoruba religion mirrored the increasing complexity of the Yoruba society. Many wise old men became priests of deities that had once represented natural forces of either the sky or earth and had many traits common to humans. In more modern times these deities came to embody the characteristics of living rulers and culture-heroes; for example, Sango, god of thunder, was once a real-life Alafin of Oyo, the secular king of all Yoruba.

These Yoruba of what is present-day Nigeria in West Africa not only recognized a very large pantheon of gods, supervised by Oludumare, the creator, but developed a highly complex yet flexible system of divination called Ifa, named after the deity who controls it. This system, evolving with typical Yoruba thoroughness and complexity to embrace any contingency, is a marvelous mix of human inventiveness and divine directive. Its very flexibility is extraordinary. It is nonjudgmental in character, therefore avoiding the traps of ethical religious systems, which produce guilt. It is a system that leaves ethical questions and concerns to the secular realm.

But much more important than a description of a religion or an analysis of its iconography, if such exists, is the question of what function that religion plays in society. Certainly that is true of the Yoruba religion and Ifa divination as it has survived successfully for at least 1,350 years. Its ability to survive seems to lie in its flexibility and its adaptability to new circumstances. Most important, however, Ifa provides a pragmatic and psychological cushion against the vicissitudes of life. To the early Yoruba people there was the ever present threat of droughts, floods, winds, baking sun, and insects, and the unseen enemies of bacteria and viruses that carried off at least three children out of every five born. Next was the terror of the Middle Passage, when so many Yoruba were sold into slavery by neighboring Yoruba kings during the internecine warfare of the late eighteenth and the nineteenth centuries.

Those who survived to reach the New World represented all specialties: priests, kings, warriors, women who were heads of huge markets, sculptors, weavers, house builders, and potters, to name but a few. Herded onto stinking ships under unspeakably horrible conditions, these Africans took with them a formidable cultural baggage of skills and knowledge invisible to their European captors, and a religion that would function to help them survive the trials and rigors of their new life.

Those Yoruba arriving in Spanish and Portuguese settlements in the New World soon found that they were forced to choose between accepting the Catholic faith or receiving crueler punishments. Sensibly, they accepted this new religion that they did not understand. Those wise *babalawos* (priests of Ifa) who survived the Middle Passage and the early days of slavery must have soon realized that it would be necessary to train apprentices in order to pass on the Yoruba religion and ensure the survival of both humans and gods. Their rationale for the survival of deities that otherwise could not cross water was that the most important spirit was Ori, the head, or rather that which was inside the head, and from that all others would come. Divination traveled intact as well.

Myths drift and change with the imaginations of the people recounting them. But increasingly in the New World, interpretation of the Yoruba religion and its rituals, as well as those of Ifa, became almost codified in a way not at all typical of Africa, where a variety of local interpretations are found to this day. Ifa divination survived fairly intact because, uncannily, it worked. Its efficacy was not just in the appropriateness of its verse but in the accumulated power of the spoken word.

This power is a phenomenon shared by a wide range of African traditions, and it has survived among peoples in the New World diaspora. Part of both the religious and the secular cultures, it is a belief that the spoken word has a power of its own, a belief that words can be spiritually potent and be protective medicine, too. Even in the secular realm of political institutions, well-spoken words can possess a kind of power over the minds of others. The praise songs voiced for deities not only make the *orisa* (or deities) happy, but the momentum of verse after verse takes on a power of its own. (It is an interesting footnote that in the New World, though the drum calls to gods are recognized, the original tonal Yoruba language, which can be plainly understood by onlookers as calls or praise songs, is not used.) The drumming that accompanies the singing of songs reinforces the power of words. Small wonder then that the power attributed to the babalawo, and the respect accorded him, comes not only from his ability to divine the messages and interpret them with the help of Orunmila (god of knowledge) through Ifa, but from his absorbing and remembering some three thousand verses associated with the various throws of the divining chain.

At the heart of this Yoruba religion is the concept of *asé,* an individual's personal spiritual power, which grows throughout life through a person's diligent application to doing good deeds, coupled with appropriate and calm behavior and with service to the gods in the form of sacrifice. The reciprocity of service between gods and humans is essentially the giving of strength, the renewal of *asé* to the orisa through blood sacrifice of animals designated as belonging to a specific deity. Renewed and grateful deities in turn bless their supportive worshipers with added *asé.* The rules of this loving support between humans and gods are all known to that father-of-all-knowledge, the babalawo.

Within the past few years, the Religion (as it is known to its devoted followers) has undergone a phenomenal surge in popularity and a metamorphosis in the United States. Santeria, the syncretism of the original Yoruba religion and Ifa with Catholicism, came into the United States first with Puerto Ricans in the forties and fifties and then with the flood of Cuban refugees in the sixties. Haitian refugees then brought Vodun, a mixture of Yoruba, Fon, and Hueda deities with Kongo gods and magic. Many practitioners of both Vodun and Santeria are now seeking the basic Yoruba religion as their priestly leaders unwind and detach the Catholic saints from the orisa. Those African Americans who reject this syncretism as a compromise to a slave religion look to Oyotunji Village near Beaufort, South Carolina, where Yoruba culture and religion is still practiced. Though some observers hail this rejection of syncretism as a rallying point for black nationalism, it seems that those who go to Oyotunji Village to study Yoruba religion (and its practice has now spread to other parts of the United States as well), are searching to reclaim the religion of strength, inner peace, and power that came out of Africa with their ancestors.

Another growing group of Ifa practitioners, of which the author of this volume is a leader, encompasses members of every race and cultural background, just as the Yoruba of Africa would have it. The island peoples of the Caribbean who brought the religion to Miami, New York, and Chicago were of both African and European backgrounds, a fact that challenges the logic of those who claim that only persons of African American descent can be part of the worship of the orisa and practice or consult with Ifa divination. Many Americans, disenchanted with Judeo-Christian religion, are seeking a religion of personal fulfillment, one that gives them a sense of personal worth and power over their own destinies. They are discovering that Ifa allows them to keep their material accomplishments while giving them a sense of spiritual release and proclaims that, if they unfetter themselves from strictly linear thinking, all things are possible.

Philip Neimark feels that Americans today are as spiritually adrift as the Africans were culturally adrift when they were brought to the shores of the New World. In a very real sense, his is a personal odyssey to discover the "why" of the success of Ifa. Along his way he has done thorough research, with some guidance from William R. Bascom, who wrote *Ifa Divination* and *Sixteen Cowries,* and from me. The result, contained in this volume, will be a handbook for all those studying the Religion. Dr. Afolabi Epega, whose introduction follows, agrees. The circle has come completely round, for it was Dr. Epega's grandfather who initiated William Bascom into Ogboni Society in Ile Ife, Nigeria, in the late 1930s and William Bascom and Melville Herskovits who directed my own field work in Nigeria.

Justine M. Cordwell, Ph.D.
May Weber Museum of Cultural Arts
Chicago, Illinois

first came into contact with Philip John Neimark/Fagbamila many years ago, when a godchild of mine in Cleveland, Ohio, called to say he was aware of a North American who was seeking to practice Ifa in the traditional fashion and thought that perhaps I would contact him. My godchild had received a copy of a newsletter written by Fagbamila from the Ifa Foundation of North America and gave me their phone number.

I called the next day, only to find that Fagbamila had been eagerly attempting to locate me for several weeks! It was as if our coming together had been preordained by the orisa. It was the beginning of a long and meaningful relationship.

As a fifth-generation African babalawo I was gratified to see our traditional religion finally spread to the United States in its original form. It was with great pride and enjoyment that I eventually initiated Fagbamila as an *oluwo,* the highest form of babalawo. Together we have performed many initiations for other Americans wishing to become priests or priestesses of the ancient religion of Ifa.

Some wonder about the propriety of a white man participating at the highest level of a "black religion." They should not question this. Ifa is not a black religion; it is an African religion originating from Ile Ife in what is now the nation of Nigeria. Oosanla, or Obatala as he is better known in the West, one of our most important orisa, was white. Ifa teaches that people of all colors were born into the earth from Ile Ife. To attempt to secularize the religion, either for personal or political purposes, is to deny the teachings of Ifa and separate yourself from the reality of the makeup of the world. Ifa teaches integrating with the world in every aspect. To segregate any part is to stray from the path. Our work and love for one another as well as our love for the sacred teachings of Ifa are living demonstration of the true reality of color and the integrative power of the orisa.

Fagbamila is a dedicated Ifa worshiper who has really experienced the way of the orisa as reflected in thoughts, words, and good deeds. His orisa-inspired teachings will help individuals develop self-respect and an elevation of character in the United States and other areas of the world. As a Western man he understands those areas in the ancient teachings most important for individuals with backgrounds similar to his own.

Afolabi Epega
Lagos, Nigeria

////////////

THE WAY OF THE ORISA

INTRODUCTION

////////////

'm no longer afraid," I replied to the *Chicago Sun-Times* reporter who asked, "What's the single most important thing that Ifa has done for you?"

I don't think I realized at the time how true that really was. The words came, as do many real truths, almost unbidden to my lips. Yet, as the years have passed I have come to understand increasingly not only the truth of my reply but its power as well. I have come to see that my fears—all fears—are burdensome and unnecessary.

I believe that fear is the primary motivating force in our culture. When I look back over my own life I see that my drive to accomplish stemmed more from a fear of what others might think of me if I *didn't* achieve than from any joy I might derive from using my inherent capabilities. I also believe that I was driven by a fear of death. If I awoke at 2:00 A.M. after downing a pizza at midnight, I was sure that I was having a heart attack rather than indigestion. If my sinuses gave me a headache, I was sure that I had a brain tumor. If I had to fly on an airplane, I worried that it would crash.

My fears were based on two faulty premises. The first was that life could be lived according to other people's standards, which is absurd. The second was that, in order to survive, I had to be in total control, which is impossible. Together, these premises provided me with more pain than pleasure.

I had been trained in an either-or notion of reality in which (or so I thought) I could choose to be material *or* spiritual but not both. But I didn't want to relinquish my worldly acquisitions or abandon my pursuits in the material world in order to have a rewarding spiritual life . . . and I didn't think I should have to.

Then, in 1974, I "discovered" Ifa, a thousands-of-years-old African religion that took root in the sophisticated city-state culture of the Yoruba kingdom in what is now Nigeria. It is the oldest monotheistic religion on earth. Ifa contains an either-or premise: in Ifa, *either* we learn to integrate the spiritual and the material *or* we can never be happy and fulfilled. Ifa does not require that we abandon our material pursuits or the pleasure and pride we take from them; in fact, it extols them. Ifa does not draw a battle line through the midbrain, pitting logic against intuition, our bodies against our souls. I think it is precisely this dichotomy, this separation of mind and spirit, that causes so much of the burnout we see in people today.

I discovered Ifa because of a whim one Sunday afternoon. My wife and I had joined some friends who were going to get a reading from a babalawo (priest). I didn't have the slightest idea what a babalawo was, and, philosophically, I was opposed to any kind of "nonsensical mysticism." All things considered, the last place you would have expected to find me on a Sunday afternoon in sunny Miami would be having my fortune told.

Yet "there are no accidents," as I have pointed out to hundreds upon hundreds of individuals who consult with me. So, on a steamy summer Sunday afternoon in Miami, Florida, I found myself being ushered into a room where three men dressed in robes and wearing strange hats were sitting cross-legged on straw mats. At the time I did not realize that this was not an everyday divination session with the local babalawo. It was divination to ascertain my personal guardian orisa and would include my first "life reading." After reciting a stream of prayers in Yoruba, the oldest babalawo began to cast the *ikin* (sacred palm nuts). He did this by passing sixteen nuts from hand to hand. If, after grabbing as many as his hand would hold, there was one nut left, he would inscribe the figure "II" in the powder on his divining tray. If two nuts were left, he would mark the figure "I." If none or three or more were left, no figure was written. After eight marks had been inscribed, my *odu,* or sign, could be interpreted.

The sum and substance of my initial reading was contained in the mythology of my sign. The story, briefly translated, tells of a young and successful ruler who was dethroned through betrayal and trickery. Not only did he lose his title; he lost his wealth, his wife, and his family and was cast out of his country into the wilderness. Here the young man tried to survive alone. He became weaker and weaker as he tried to battle the elements without shelter or tools.

In a neighboring kingdom, much larger and more prosperous than the one from which the young king had been exiled, an aged king had passed away. The babalawos, in casting for a new *oba* (king), had related to the people of the kingdom that Orunmila (orisa of knowledge) had foretold that the new *oba* would be found alone and naked where a plume of smoke appeared.

Back in the wilderness the young man sat shivering and alone. He had given up all hope of ever returning to his kingdom, and he was fast losing his confidence in his ability to survive long enough to reach a neighboring land. Finally, with great sadness, the young man removed the last vestiges of his former greatness, his royal robes. Placing them in a pile, he set fire to them and huddled close to the flame for the warmth he so desperately needed.

The babalawos from the neighboring kingdom looked out into the jungle and saw a single plume of black smoke rising skyward. They rushed toward the site, and there, as Orunmila had foretold, was a young naked man. The prophecy had come to pass. The young man was made *oba* of the new kingdom, and his greatness, his wealth, his wives, and his family were more abundant than ever.

In interpreting this for me, the babalawo concluded the following: First, I would probably lose much of what I had achieved up to that point. Second, if I sacrificed and followed Orunmila, I would become greater than ever before. Third, to ultimately realize the full potential of my path, it was imperative that I become a babalawo! Indeed, I would lose all I had acquired so that I could search out my correct path. Oh yes, my guardian orisa was Obatala.

It was the last thing in the world I wanted to hear, and I didn't believe it. I was thirty-three years old, rich, and successful. That three little men sitting on a straw mat could tell me that all that would change was ridiculous.

One year later, most of what they had warned about had come to pass.

I remember my reluctance to accept that what had happened was anything but a coincidence or self-fulfilling prophecy. I even contacted the Western world's foremost authority on Ifa, Dr. William Bascom, professor of anthropology at the University of California at Berkeley, who after almost an hour on the phone, left me more confused than ever. I remember my frustration at not being able to get a "rational" explanation for what had happened and finally blurted out, "Dr. Bascom, you sound as if you believe in it!" His response, which was to change my life, was simply "Mr. Neimark, all I can tell you is, *it works.*"

Opon, or diviner's tray, with tapper.

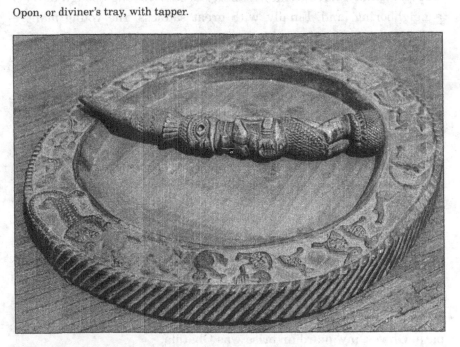

The Cartesian worldview has shaped every aspect of our lives, holding that all things can be broken down into parts (the body is a group of atoms, for example), which thereby enables us to believe that we can master each component and, subsequently, the whole. This worldview has set up a world of either-ors—the dualism that has created such a dangerous imbalance in our lives and the life of the planet.

In Ifa, it is understood that, as with logic and intuition, the rational and nonrational, linear and nonlinear were given to us to use and to use together. To Ifa, the singular excesses of materialism are as unintelligent as the singular excesses of spirituality. To use only one half of your capacity—either half—is to play at life with half a deck.

From its inception, Ifa has been based on an undeniable pragmatism. We believe in results. Through its ancient rituals and prayers, Ifa shows us that it is not only permissible but imperative that we use our spiritual capacities to favorably influence our everyday lives. And why not? Ifa recognizes the universal need for secure *and* fulfilling lives and gives us rules and rituals for tapping into the great pool of unquenchable energy to solve our problems and make practical improvements. We do this through ancestor worship, divination, and the orisa.

One of the central beliefs of Ifa is that only two events in our lives are predetermined: the day we are born and the day we are supposed to die. Everything else, without exception, can be forecast and, when necessary, changed!

Ifa understands that we are part of this universe in a literal, not a figurative, way. As parts of this incredibly intricate organism we call the universe, we all contain minute quantities of the energy that exists all around us. By learning the instructions for accessing that energy, we can make the most dramatic and profound changes in our lives—real, objective changes.

I have written this book to provide you with instructions on practice as well as to describe the richness and beauty that Ifa can bring into your life, as it did mine. Part One gives a brief overview of the philosophy and basic practices of Ifa. Chapters on ancestor worship, death and rebirth, divination, and sacrifice will give you a basic understanding of Ifa so that you can begin to sense its power. Part Two invites you to learn, use, and connect with the real and practical energy of the orisa, or guardian spirits. You will learn to identify your own personal guardian orisa and learn how to effectively use its energy to change and improve your life.

Remember, Ifa is a journey, not a destination. Growth, wisdom, and personal fulfillment are its mile markers. Ifa has allowed me to thrive in the material and spiritual worlds. It has become my path. It can work for you, too. May this book be your road map.

Ko Si Ku

Ko Si Arun

Ko Si Eyo

Ko Si Ofo

Ko Si Idina

Ariku Babawa.

So that death is no more

Sickness is no more

Tragedy is no more

Loss is no more

Obstacle is no more

Don't let us see the death of our father.

SIXTEEN TRUTHS OF IFA

1. There is a single God.

2. There is no Devil.

3. Except for the day you were born and the day you are supposed to die, there is no single event in your life that cannot be forecast and, when necessary, changed.

4. It is your birthright to be happy, successful, and fulfilled.

5. You should grow and obtain wisdom during the process.

6. You are reborn through your blood relatives.

7. Heaven is "home" and Earth "the marketplace." We are in constant passage between the two.

8. You are part of the universe in a literal, not figurative, way.

9. You must never initiate harm to another human being.

10. You must never harm the universe of which you are part.

11. Your temporal and spiritual capacities must work together.

12. You are born with a specific path. It is your goal to travel it. Divination provides your road map.

13. Our ancestors exist and must be honored.

14. Sacrifice guarantees success.

15. The orisa live within us.

16. You need have no fear.

PART ONE

THE WAY OF IFA

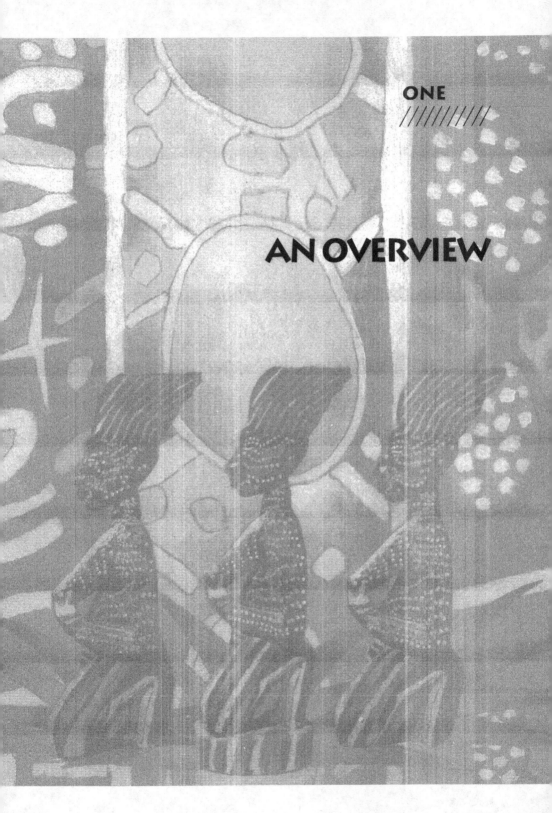

ONE
//////////

AN OVERVIEW

believe that the sole reason for the existence of any formal religious philosophy is to teach transcendence. Just as our universities teach us how to access and be comfortable with the logical capacities of our brains, formal religion should be the University of the Spirit. In the same way that we learn how to balance our checkbooks, run a computer, or repair a car by using the logical hemisphere of the brain, religion should teach us how to use the intuitive hemisphere to access the energy and power that exist only in the nonlinear world. To reach transcendence—that simple but exquisite act of feeling, unencumbered by any linear thought—is the key. Ifa is one of the oldest universities of the spirit and has for thousands of years taught how to effectively access the energy of transcendence and use it *with* logical behavior in a productive fashion.

The philosophy of Ifa originated with the Yoruba peoples of West Africa in what is now Nigeria. Ifa mythology relates that the creation of humankind arose in the sacred city of Ile Ife just outside what is now Lagos. The Yoruba created a highly sophisticated city-state empire, which, according to many anthropologists, was on a par with that of ancient Athens. Their philosophy reflected an integration of the basic truths and wisdom of nature with the equally true, but vastly different, demands of a sophisticated commercial culture. Ifa was not a product of superstition, ignorance, or lack of education but of years of practice and refinement by successful, intelligent, and highly educated men and women who used it for the simplest of reasons: it worked!

Indeed, my original fascination with Ifa was based, in large measure, on trying to understand how this philosophy could have survived for thousands of years if it had to provide practical, everyday results for its followers. You either cure the illness or you don't. You either get the job or you don't. You either win the dispute or you don't. These are not the kind of results that can be hedged or put off "until you are ready" or until your next life.

And then I saw the barren have children, business disaster turn to success, and "incurable" illnesses cured through divination and sacrifice. I have come to believe that Oludumare (God) understands that belief is easier to acquire when there are practical results. So he not only provides his followers with the instructions for improving their lives, he intends for them to substantiate their faith through practical, everyday results.

The basic foundation of Ifa is three-pronged: orisa worship, ancestor worship, and divination.

THE ORISA

The orisa are energy that, for the most part, represent aspects of nature. Osun (pronounced O-SHUN) represents sweet waters, love, money, conception; Sango (pronounced Zhan-GO) represents thunder and lightning, strategy, and he is the warrior; Esu (pronounced A-shew), messenger to Oludumare (the single God), owner of roads and opportunities, owner of *asé* (spiritual energy); Yemonja/Olukun (pronounced Yeh-MO-zha/O-lu-KUN), the ocean, mother, provider of wealth; Obatala (pronounced O-BA-ta-la), the head, clarity, arbiter of justice; Oya (pronounced Oi-YA!), marketplace, tornadoes, change of fortune, she is the female warrior; Ogun, owner of all metals, fierce warrior, honor, and integrity.

As parts of one intricate universal body, we all contain minute portions of the energies from all its other parts. In the worldview of Ifa, in addition to being primarily human, we are also the rock, the lion, the tree, the ocean. Through the worship of orisa, we can each take our own small quantity of the other types of energy and loop it to its concomitant energies in nature. For example, a woman unable to conceive a child would most likely find it necessary to tap into the energy of Osun, orisa of sweet water, love, money, and conception. Someone suffering from a troubled head, or too much pressure from work, would find it productive to tap into the energy of Obatala, orisa of the head, justice, coolness, and clear thinking. By calling upon the orisa, we are able to geometrically increase our power to change or improve specific situations in our lives.

Ifa also teaches that each of us has a single orisa energy from the universe that is predominant within us. We call this our guardian orisa. Learning to be comfortable with its characteristics and to tap into them in a meaningful way is an important step toward successfully traveling our paths. In Part Two, I will guide you to identification of your own guardian orisa.

ANCESTOR WORSHIP

Ancestor worship is a formalized structure for connecting with the accumulated knowledge, wisdom, and power of our dead blood relatives. Ifa understands that energy—the essence of us all—cannot be created or destroyed. The energy and wisdom of our deceased blood relatives is uniquely connected with and available to us. It is not simply RNA or DNA that links us to our past; it is a road of energy and power that is available to those of us who know and practice the rituals.

DIVINATION

In Ifa, we believe that our destinies or life patterns are established prior to our births into this world, and that through information obtained through divination, it is possible to know something about our futures and the outcomes of all of our undertakings. We believe that we can improve upon these life patterns with proper offerings and devotions.

Ifa teaches that, with the exception of the day you are born and the day you are supposed to die, there is no single event that cannot be forecast and, when necessary, changed. Anything less would imply predestination, which is antithetical to the Ifa concept that we "crown our own heads."

Unlike other paradigms such as astrology, I Ching, or tarot, Ifa divination tells us what is likely to happen if we do *nothing* to change our circumstance. Not only does it forecast the future, it offers an opportunity to change it! By identifying a potential problem or potential good fortune, the babalawo can pinpoint the energy source necessary to alter or enhance it as well as provide the client with a specific ritual for accessing the energy (orisa) that will help accomplish the task.

The first, and most important, method of divination is that performed through the use of *ikin,* a kind of palm nut that is thrown to obtain a series of eight binary symbols. These symbols, called *odus,* can almost be considered chapter headings in the sacred book of Ifa divination. Each odu refers to specific tales that have been passed on from one babalawo to another for thousands of years in an oral tradition.

The babalawo will ascertain the specific odus that represent a client's current situation through a reading of the eight binary numbers. This initial reading will reveal which primary odu is operative for the client at that moment. Then, through a series of alternative casts, he can select the particular story that is most pertinent to the client's needs. Skilled babalawos understand that the genuine or core issue affecting a client is often not the problem for which the client sought help. For example, a man may come to the babalawo because business is bad and he is feeling financial strain. His reading, however, might indicate that his problems are with his family and that it is *that* stress that is creating disruption to his energy flow, thereby causing him to neglect or do an inadequate job at work. The knowledgeable babalawo can see the root problem and suggest ways to correct it. The secondary problems will then resolve themselves.

It is important to differentiate between the odu's call for sacrifices, or *ebos,* in order to alleviate specific problems or conditions and the overview of the odu itself. In one sense the problems, potential dangers, or good fortune indicated during divination represent the potholes or unexpected rewards on a person's path. Although the roadblocks must be removed, what the client really needs is to see his or her true life's path. This concept is best expressed in a Yoruba saying:

Eniti o ru bo ti ko
gba ewo bi eni f'owo
ebo s'ofil o ri.

One who offers sacrifice but does not observe the taboo
is no better off than if he had thrown away the money
he spent on the sacrifice.

The second method of divination used by the babalawo employs the *opele,* a chain containing eight halfseed shells that with a single toss will provide the eight symbols necessary to identify the one odu that applies to the client's problems or needs. In common practice, the *opele* is used for "everyday" problems, whereas the *ikin* is used for initiation and for serious issues.

A babalawo from Benin City, Nigeria, c. 1950.

THE HARMONY OF THE SPIRITUAL AND MATERIAL

Ifa functions on the basic principle that our spiritual and worldly sides are not separate and competing entities. We believe that in order for either to succeed, they must work together.

We are neither born of sin nor born with guilt. Our only inherent obligation is to make the most of our potential. If a person wishes to be rich (and Ifa recognizes worldly goods as a blessing), that's fine. If another wishes to help the needy, that's fine, too. In Ifa, it does not matter what you choose to do; what matters is how you do it. If you do it well, in harmony with the universe, and in conjunction with your destiny, you will learn and grow along the way. Ifa offers you the possibility of joy and fulfillment. Growth and wisdom are your obligations.

Ifa, for the most part, is loath to involve us in absolute moral truths. We do not believe that God commanded, "Thou shalt not steal" or "Thou shalt not cut down the rain forest" or "Thou shall not covet thy neighbor's mate." God gave us brains, and Ifa works on the principle that we are expected to use them! We would not cut down old-growth trees because our children or grandchildren might not have any air to breathe if we did. We don't steal or have sexual relationships with our neighbor's mate because if we did, we would create or perpetuate a climate in which our own property or our mate is fair game for others.

In Ifa, we believe in using common sense in an integrated and rational fashion. Using only our rational or only our spiritual sides will invariably lead to bad results. We reject a dichotomy of mind and spirit and embrace the concept that the linear and nonlinear, practical and spiritual, analytical and emotional components of our beings are neither separate nor antithetical. They are partners supporting the joyous process of living a full and wise life in harmony with the universe.

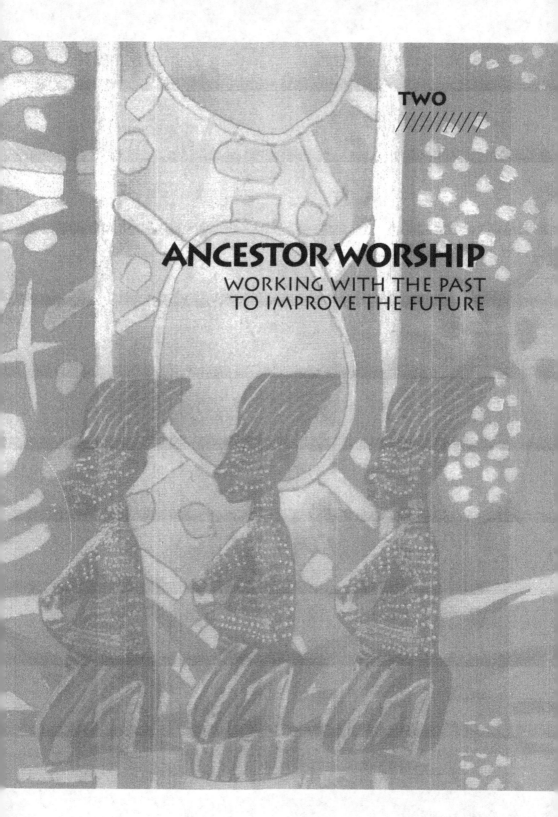

TWO

ANCESTOR WORSHIP
WORKING WITH THE PAST
TO IMPROVE THE FUTURE

The importance of ancestor worship lies in the knowledge it provides us that our current existence is not "all there is."

Ifa's worldview can be thought of as the spiritual representation of Einstein's theory of relativity. Our belief in, and practice of, ancestor worship bridges the time gap that Einstein believed must exist between the past, present, and future. In Ifa, we understand that the invisible world of our deceased ancestors combines with the visible world of nature and human culture to form a single organic truth. Through ritual we bridge the relationship between the past and the present and in the process improve the future. The ritual process of ancestor worship can provide us with profound, quantifiable changes in our everyday lives. But the concept often meets with resistance.

For example, several years ago I saw a client who was in her early forties and had received her Ph.D. in philosophy from the University of Chicago. She was both academically and personally interested in nontraditional forms of divination. Her personal "project" was a book on astrology from an academician's viewpoint. She was immediately attracted to the beauty and power of Ifa and within just a few short months had received her warriors (Esu, Ososi, Ogun, and Osun) and had undergone several other small initiation rites. Time and again she marveled at the connection she felt and the power Ifa offered. She was so enamored of what she felt that she told me she wished to become a priestess of Yemonja/Olukun, her guardian orisa.

During this period she came for divination frequently. With a single exception she followed all the prescribed sacrifices and offerings. The one exception was that she would not offer prayers and food to the spirit of her dead father. The first time she was called upon to do it she made no mention of her inner conflicts. But Ifa simply won't let you slide, so the necessity of ancestor worship—and of dealing with her departed father in particular—began to appear in every reading.

Finally, she exploded: "Phil, he was a no-good so-and-so; he berated me my whole life. Most of my problems have been a direct result of his unfeeling and uncaring behavior. I'll be damned if I'll offer him my love now!" I wasn't particularly shocked. Many of us have had trouble with relatives now deceased, but I did want her to understand the imperative of following the readings.

"First," I replied, "there is no point in fighting with the dead. Second, no matter what kind of an SOB your father was when he was alive, there are two facts you have to understand: first, you wouldn't be here without him, and second, whatever he 'was' he 'isn't' anymore! That trip is over, those experiences simply a small addition to the experiences of previous lifetimes. Now, instead of carrying all that negative energy, which impedes your growth and progress, instead of continuing to deny the love you were never allowed to express, you can make up and go forward with your life. And the way to do that is to finally tell him how much love you had for him and how much love you

Orisa figures at the main shrine, Oshogbo, Nigeria, 1950.

needed. I know it will be difficult, probably cathartic, but Ifa is saying that unless you disperse the negative energy you'll remain blocked and unfulfilled. The only way to get through that pain is by expressing the love that caused it. If you hadn't cared, hadn't loved your father, hadn't needed to be loved in return, you wouldn't feel all this rage and pain. When he died, you probably thought it was 'over.' It isn't! You probably felt it was too late for anything to be done. It isn't! It's time to do it and get on with your life. It's time to be loved by him in return."

Three days later, on a Sunday morning, she called to tell me that she was "opting out." I explained that you couldn't "opt out" of life, you could only choose to live it fully or not. But the choice was hers. Regardless of her decision, she had our love and compassion. Her experience, while extreme, is not atypical of the difficulty many of us have in coming to grips with our ancestors.

My good friend and teacher Afolabi Epega, like the woman above, also has his Ph.D. His is in chemistry. Afolabi is also a fifth-generation babalawo whose grandfather was perhaps the most famous babalawo in written history. The first time we discussed ancestor worship, Afolabi simply told me the following story:

I was in the midst of preparing a paper on some of the histories that comprise the sacred odu, when I suddenly could not remember one particular story. The paper was due in just three days. In your country you might pick up the phone and call someone to find the information, but in truth, these facts were known only by my father, who lived in Lagos, and my deceased grandfather. At that time Nigeria still did not have phones in many individual homes, so contacting my father prior to presentation of my paper would be impossible. Unless I restructured my entire lecture I would have to find the missing history. So, I "called" my grandfather in our way. I used our ritual of ancestor worship to convey to him that I needed his help. The next night, I awakened from a sound sleep to see my grandfather sitting on the edge of my bed. "What is the problem Falo?" he asked. I explained my situation, and he instructed me to get a pencil and paper that I keep near my nightstand. He proceeded to give me the information I had forgotten. When he was finished I expressed my love and gratitude to him, and he expressed his to me. I fell back into a deep sleep. The next morning I awoke with vague memories of the night before, but they seemed more dreamlike than real until I glanced at my nightstand and saw the writing there. Then I remembered my grandfather's visit. I was able to quickly complete my paper and give a thorough presentation to the class.

For almost 96 percent of the world's population, ritual offerings and prayers to deceased blood relatives are an integral part of everyday life. People of Eastern cultures such as the Chinese, Koreans, Indians, Japanese, and Tibetans, along with great segments of the populations of South America, Mexico, Cuba, Bali, Indonesia, Polynesia, Mongolia, the Eastern Baltics, Iceland, and New Guinea offer respect to and seek guidance from their ancestors. Yet because most of us in the Western world were raised in the Jewish and Christian traditions, which proscribe ancestor worship, Western newcomers to Ifa tend to be skeptical of it. Ancestor worship fits perfectly into the Ifa devotee's integrated view of the physical and spiritual worlds.

You would imagine that everyone would be thrilled to have "proof," or a way to authenticate knowledge, of an afterlife. If you were to ask one hundred "average" Americans if they believe in life after death, one or two might say yes. Five or ten will say absolutely not. But about ninety percent will tell you, "Well, I'd like to, but I really don't know." Yet when Ifa offers them a way to "know," they still resist.

Let me explain what I mean by knowledge. Knowledge is what you really know in your heart or in your gut. It's not always logical, but it is totally real and true. A mother, for example, "knows" that she loves her child. If someone or something starts to hurt that child, she will instantly, automatically, and without "thinking" do anything in her power to protect it. Even if the child misbehaves, or grows up and ignores her, that love will not waver. Knowledge comes from feeling and experience. It is not quantifiable. You know when you love another person; you know when you are moved by a book, music, or a sunset; you know when you feel peaceful—not because someone has listed all the good characteristics of the person you love or explained the sentence structure in the book, the mathematical precision of the music, or the light waves of the sunset, but because you experience it, you feel it. Logic has nothing to do with it. In fact, the truth of knowing something is much more powerful, accurate, and trustworthy than the linear processes of "learning" or "understanding."

Ancestor worship will provide you with the knowledge that life is a continuum by enabling you to actually communicate with the energy of your departed family members and feel the profound feelings that that engenders. This may not happen in a familiar form—you may not find your grandfather sitting on the edge of your bed—but it will nonetheless be real and true. Not a product of wish fulfillment or hysteria, it will come through as irrefutable knowledge of the nonlinear side of reality.

Why are we so afraid of this knowledge? The answer, I believe, is that when we actually experience this access to other worlds, we are forced to question the very foundations and premises upon which we have built our lives—questions that invite change. And humans are naturally resistant to change.

Try to imagine the kinds of decisions you would make if you knew you would have future lives. Think about the number of short-term choices you make now. After all, if you believe that this is your only time around, then it makes sense to cram it with gratification and sensation. Growth and development would seem less important than acquisition and indulgence. The national debt, environmental destruction, pollution, the elimination of plant and animal species, fast cars, and fast food—all are products of our culture's fixation on the now. But if you knew this wasn't your only time around, you would be far less likely to cut down the rain forest, use nonrenewable resources, or poison the rivers and oceans with lethal waste. Laws won't stop you from tossing a junk food bag out of your car window, but understanding that you need a healthy Earth for your own long-term survival not only might stop you from tossing the bag but would probably stop you from abusing your body with fast food in the first place.

Through ancestor worship, Ifa allows you to experience life as a continuum. And once you have, nothing will ever be the same again. The same kind of attitude changes and life changes that have affected nearly every individual who has gone through what we call a near-death experience, who has experienced the other dimension and then been brought back, testifies to the effect of this knowledge. One does not have to die and be brought back to experience it; ancestor worship is our connection to the past and our road map to a better future.

HOW IT IS DONE

The actual ritual of ancestor worship is extremely simple. For the basic ritual all you need is a clear glass, natural water, a white candle, and the discipline to set aside thirteen minutes a day for seven consecutive days. For seven consecutive days, at the exact same time each day, you will light the candle and offer prayers to your blood ancestors. You will call each name three times, and, after offering your love and your thanks, after offering the water for coolness and refreshment and the candle for light and energy, you may bring your problems to them. This doesn't mean asking them for a new pair of shoes or for your lover to call that night. We only ask our ancestors to intervene in serious life situations. The loss of a job, illness, the breakup of a relationship— these are the kinds of issues for which it is proper to ask their help. If no serious problems exist, then simply ask them for guidance in your life, health for you and those you love, and prosperity for your home.

For example, my prayers go something like this:

Ajuba (blessings) to all my departed ancestors. Particular blessings and thankfulness to my father, Mortimer Neimark, my father, Mortimer Neimark, my father, Mortimer Neimark. Also to my mother, Hortense Neimark, Hortense Neimark, Hortense Neimark; to my son Adam Neimark, Adam Neimark, Adam Neimark, and to all my children who did not reach term; to my grandparents John and Lillian Peters, John and Lillian Peters, John and Lillian Peters; Charles and Etta Neimark, Charles and Etta Neimark, Charles and Etta Neimark; to my great un- cles Stanley Neimark, Stanley Neimark, Stanley Neimark, Arthur Peters, Arthur Peters, Arthur Peters, Norman Peters, Norman Peters, Norman Peters; to my great aunts Genevieve Neimark, Genevieve Neimark, Genivieve Neimark, and Lucy Ribback Peters, Lucy Ribback Peters, Lucy Ribback Peters; to my great-grandmother Nancy Peters, Nancy Peters, Nancy Peters, as well as all those whose names I do not know but whose blood runs through my veins. Please accept the coolness of this water so that you may be cool and comfortable. Please accept the light and energy so that you may have brightness and strength. I love and miss your presence here on Earth but gather strength and wisdom from your continued energy and guidance. May that guidance continue to open my paths and roads and the paths and roads of those I love. May your strength and energy give health to me and those I love. May your wisdom bring love and prosperity into my home.

This is simply an outline, and I think you'll find that if a lot is going on in your life, your prayers will be more complex. Also, the setting can be much more elaborate. Most priests I know put a table in one corner of a room and place as many photographs of their ancestors on it as possible. *A quick word of caution:* the pictures should contain only deceased relatives; it is acceptable for you to appear in the pictures but not any other living being lest he or she join the deceased. You might place some of your ancestors' favorite items on the table, too. For example, my shrine has Parliament cigarettes for my mother and father, cards for all those who played bridge and other games, coffee for them all, along with an occasional cigar, fruit, candy, honey, or anything else I feel they might appreciate.

Be aware that when you take a specific problem to your ancestors, the solution may come in many forms. It is possible one of your ancestors will appear in your dreams and offer a suggestion or solution. Perhaps you will suddenly get a flash or insight into the problem, or perhaps the problem will simply cease to exist for no apparent reason. So when you are asking your ancestors for help, it is important to be open and aware and to keep a pencil and paper by your bed so that when you awaken from a dream, you can jot it down before it fades into the morning.

A few answers to the questions I know you will have:

Do I let the candle burn?

You can, but it is not necessary. You can put the candle out after the thirteen minutes and relight it the next day.

Do I keep giving new water?

No. The fresh natural water (bottled spring water, for example) should be placed on the shrine and allowed to slowly evaporate over the seven days. This symbolizes your ancestors' drinking.

Do I have to do it at night?

No. You may do it any time of the day or night. But, if you start at 6:00 A.M. you must do it at exactly 6:00 A.M. each of the seven days. If you "blow it," you start over.

Can I do it for a lesser or greater number of days?

Within our belief system there are occasions for performing worship for three days, fourteen days, seventeen days, and twenty-one days. These are for specific and highly esoteric reasons. Ninety-nine percent of the time, seven days is the correct number.

Do I have to have pictures?

No. You don't even have to have a formal shrine. All you need is the water, candle, and your prayers.

What happens if I'm traveling?

If you leave during the course of the seven days, simply continue the sequence wherever you are staying. Be sure to adjust the time to when you were doing it at home. For example, if you were praying each night at 11:14 P.M. in Chicago, you would pray at 12:14 A.M. in New York or 9:14 P.M. in Los Angeles. Remember, you can do it anywhere—at your friend's home, at Howard Johnson's, or at your summer cottage.

Can I keep a candle going all the time?

Yes. You may work with your shrine in any way you like. You can replenish the fruits and drinks and presents daily or weekly, as do most people around the world. The formal worship, however, takes place on seven consecutive days within each month. The only exception to that would be if you had a reading from a babalawo indicating that some other approach was necessary in order to solve a specific problem.

I had a friend who was as close or closer to me than my relatives. I called her "aunt." Can she be included in my worship?

No! Only blood relatives can be worshiped in this way.

Ancestor worship is one-third of the power of Ifa. It requires no initiation, no conversion, no expense. It is something that everyone can do. It is a powerful tool for making positive and discernible changes in our lives. It is equally effective in providing us with the awareness that life is not a single, accidental event but a continuing process that offers endless possibilities and pleasures.

THREE

SACRIFICE

*Para Oluku oko, Odede, Oluko
Ada li o difa f'Orunmila nigbi
oun mi bowa si ode aye won ni
koniite titi. Ewure, eku ati eja li
ebo. Orunmila gbo ebo o ru, nito
naa lati igbati a ti da aye,
Orunmila ko te titi o fidi oni oloni
yi. Orunmila lioda ile, Oun lioko
tee. Oun li o ko awon Awo ni Eko
Ifa tiosifi awon odu si aye won si
besibe oun kiiko etyididi si ebo
tiaba yan fun un nito to oun ti
fihan gbogbo eda alaaye pe: A
kiigbaisebo ki ara kioro ni.*

*Nibi pupo ninu Eko Ifa li a si nri
apeere rere re pe: Omo eniyan ko
le gbaisebo ki ara ki o roo. ati pe:
Ebo kekeke nii ngba alaiku la.
Eniti o ba si ni ire liomaa ns ebo,
eniti o basi feran iwa ooresise
paapaa fun awon alaini, oun
paapaa ko niiye ni idunnu.*

Para, the friend of the hoe Oko
and Odede, the friend of the cutlass Ada, divined for Orunmila
while coming to the world. He
was told he would never come
into disrepute. He was to offer a
she goat, a rat and a fish as sacrifice, which he did; hence up till
today Orunmila's reputation
flourishes. Orunmila created the
Earth. He first trod on it; he
trained the disciples and set all
the odus in their respective
places. Not withstanding all this
he never failed to sacrifice, because he had demonstrated to
human beings A kiigbaisebo ki
ara ki oro'ni

(Throughout the teachings of Ifa
it has been clearly expressed that
human beings cannot live peacefully without sacrifices.) Little
sacrifices avert premature death.
Making sacrifices always guarantees success.

—OGBETURA

acrifice is an avenue for restoring whatever positive process has been disrupted in your life *and* for acquiring general well-being from Oludumare (our God). There are three kinds of sacrifice—*ebo, etutu,* and *ipese.*

EBO

Simply stated, ebos are the practical offerings of sacrificial elements to the orisa, the divine designates who carry our pleas or wishes to Oludumare. For example, offerings may be made to Ogun, Obatala, Esu, Ifa, Osun, Ori. The specific offerings one would make to a particular orisa would depend upon the problem being approached and the orisa to be appeased. In Part Two, I will recommend specific ebos for each orisa.

ETUTU

Etutu are offerings to our ancestors, or *egungun.* Ifa believes that no matter what we do in life, supporting our ancestors is essential. It is through *etutu* that spiritual linkage is achieved. Ifa urges us to be in constant spiritual communication with our *egungun.*

IPESE

Ipese are the forms of sacrifice offered to *aje* (witches) and *ajogun* (both good and bad energies controlled by the orisa Esu). These offerings are commonly left at *orita* (crossroads). Ifa believes that witches and wizards are living human beings like you and me, and it is for this reason that their offerings are usually placed in open spaces frequented by humans.

As confirmed by the following sacred Ifa odu (prayer), when sacrifice is made, we unconsciously send the orisa and Ori Apere (the spirit controlling destiny) on spiritual errands. These errands are beyond human comprehension but protect us from the evil machinations of the *ajogun* and *aje*.

Sakiti ni ngboju aro

Ikasi omini o kan boroboro

Ogun ajaju ni o j'omo o m ojo orori baba

Ogun ajaju ni o j'omo o m oju orori yeye

A difa fun Ogunnulola i yoo loyun Osanyin sinu

Igbati yoo bi o bi Egbe

O'bi ajabo [or owo]

O'bi afeiri [or isiju]

O wa bi Ebo tii se omo ikehin won lenjelenje

Nijo o buro, egbe rebi, Egbe o si nile

Ajabo o tile si nile rara

Ojo o buro, Ebo nii gbe ni yo.

Sakiti (film) covers the local dye

Water drawn overnight never sours easily

Continuous war prevents the child from knowing his father's grave

Continuous war prevents the child from knowing his mother's
    grave

Divined for Ogunnulola when conceived of Osonyin

Ogunnulola gave birth to Egbe [power to disappear from sight]

Ogunnulola gave birth to Ajabo [power of safety in turbulence]

Ogunnulola gave birth to Afeiri [power of invisibility]

Ogunnulola gave birth to Ebo [sacrifice]

On a turbulent day Egbe traveled

On a turbulent day, Ajabo left permanently on tour

On a turbulent day, Afeiri was nowhere to be found

In turbulence it is Ebo [sacrifice] that saves.

Sacrifice is essential to human well-being. Literally thousands of items are used as offerings, including money, fruit, liquor, kola nuts, palm oil, shea butter, knives, mats, and virtually anything else that may appeal to a particular orisa or the *aje* and *ajogun*. On occasions when the problem is severe, when the life or death of an individual is at stake, or when initiation is to take place, the sacrifice will invariably include the offering of blood. This disturbs Americans more than any other aspect of Ifa and is often the thing they seize upon to dismiss the whole. Indeed, in the close to three years I spent trying to gain religious status and approval for exemption from the IRS and the Justice Department, the most difficult hurdle I had to overcome was their apprehension about blood sacrifice. Ultimately they acted fairly and granted my Ifa Foundation of North America full religious status.

My personal experience has been that nobody, no matter how "morally" opposed to animal sacrifice, will hesitate for one moment to avail themselves of its power when all other approaches have failed. The mother whose child is dying, the individual about to lose a job or a business, or the man or woman facing a potentially devastating court case will have absolutely no qualms about using blood sacrifice to solve apparently insoluble problems.

We use specific animals for specific problems:

▲ Sheep and pigeons for long life

▲ Hen or female goat to get a wife

▲ Rooster, male goat, or ram to get a husband

▲ Rooster, male goat, or ram to overcome enemies

▲ Rooster, male goat, or ram for good health

▲ Pigeons for money, particularly eight white doves to Obatala

▲ Hen or female goat for children

▲ Rooster, male goat, or ram for court cases

▲ Ram, male goat, rooster, or tortoise to prevent misfortune

▲ Pig, guinea fowl, or fish to become prosperous

▲ Ducks, roosters, hens, or female goats for many children and grandchildren

Like most Americans, my experience with death, before my involvement with Ifa, had always been somewhat surreal. Death was something to be avoided. Everything from our funerals to our supermarkets are designed to camouflage or disguise death. Whereas my great-grandmother may have gone out in the yard, grabbed a hen, wrung its neck, plucked its feathers, and prepared it for dinner, my only experience with dead animals was seeing them in the refrigerator case at our local supermarket. The chicken or the roast, carefully wrapped in its Styrofoam packaging, bears little resemblance to the living animal from which it came. So too, with funerals. We distance ourselves from death. Embalming removes all traces of blood, and the departed is made up and dressed to appear as "lifelike" as possible. That's the way we want it.

We intentionally block awareness that the body of someone who has died is simply an empty container. Instead we cling to the "body" as the thing—even if it is void of life and energy. Death is the ultimate enemy, so we pretend it doesn't exist. Ifa understands that you cannot be truly alive unless and until you understand death. And animal sacrifice is part of that understanding.

Blood sacrifice, as frightening and abhorrent as it is to those who do not understand it, is absolutely necessary if major change is to take place. It would be far easier for a twentieth-century European babalawo such as myself to simply say, "Blood sacrifice may have been relevant or acceptable hundreds or thousands of years ago, but in today's 'enlightened' world, simple offerings of fruit or wine will suffice." It would be far easier, but it would be untrue.

In Ifa we sacrifice only to improve or save people's lives. We value the lives of animals, but we value the lives of humans more. When an animal sacrifice is called for, the animal is offered with respect, prayer, and as little pain as possible. We understand what the animal is giving up for us, and we are grateful. For those who have forgotten, this was the very message we were to derive from the death of Jesus— that through his sacrifice our lives would be improved. I can assure you that the animals that occupy the sterile, environmentally polluting packages in your supermarket were not treated with respect or offered in prayer. To the Ifa devotee, that, and not animal sacrifice, is senseless slaughter.

I think that part of our fear of sacrifice is actually fear of feelings. In our culture, we use the left (linear) hemisphere of our brains almost exclusively, rarely allowing ourselves to experience profound feelings of any kind. We tend to live in an emotional middle zone. In so doing, we may ward off intense pain, but we also give up the opportunity for intense pleasure. When we witness or take part in an animal sacrifice, it is not possible to modulate or contain our feelings. I believe that it is the fear of that kind of intensity and what it will do, more than actual concern about the death of the animal, that shapes most people's attitudes about sacrifice.

They're not wrong. The act of animal sacrifice *is* pure feeling and energy, and no one participating in one can fail to be touched and changed from its power. But that is the point. Since the beginning of time, in every culture and every religion, sacrifice has been used to access that world of power. It cannot be intellectualized. It can only be experienced.

Though animal rights activists who disapprove of what we do undoubtedly mean well, I believe that they are in denial of death. In their zeal to "protect," they defend themselves against the heightened emotion that accompanies any thoughts of death. Ifa works *with* these emotions, in harmony with and respect for the planet. We would never needlessly harm an animal. We would never, under any circumstances, sacrifice an endangered species. When it becomes necessary to offer a rooster, goat, sheep, or pigeon for the life or well-being of another human, it is done with reverence and respect . . . for the animal *and* the individual. Without that mutual respect, the babalawo, no matter how skilled or learned, can accomplish very little. One must understand the threads of the universe if one hopes to rearrange them.

In Ifa, blood sacrifice is usually undertaken only for major problems and for initiation. When an animal has been used to remove illness or misfortune, its flesh is not eaten. When an animal is offered as part of the process of initiation or for the enhancement of some joyous moment such as childbirth, marriage, or the opening of a new business, the animal will be skinned and prepared for cooking. The meat of that animal is thought to carry powerful *asé,* or energy, and is good for all who partake. In this, Ifa is very similar to the Hebraic concept of kosher. The animal is made kosher when the rabbi lets its blood while offering prayers to God. The act of making something kosher was not intended to be restrictive but rather transcendent; the individual eating the kosher food is supposed to acquire the spirituality of the sacrifice itself. And as in the Jewish tradition, in Ifa only a trained holy person (babalawo, or priest) who has been initiated into the use of the knife can perform the ceremonies.

I attended my first animal sacrifice about a year after my first reading. I was about to receive Yemonja/Olukun, a major Yoruba orisa, and the ceremony involved animal sacrifice. When the animals were brought in and the babalawo reached for his knife, a kind of horrible dread rushed through me. I couldn't identify exactly what it was, but it was some combination of dread and wonder at what my own reaction would be. Would I get sick to my stomach? Would I get dizzy or faint? Would I have nightmares afterward? These and dozens of similar fears ran through my mind as I forced myself to watch. Then the babalawo motioned for me to come forward. He had taken the head of the animal and was holding it firmly between his hands.

"Philip," he said, "I want you to touch your forehead to the forehead of the animal. I want you to thank the animal for giving his life for you, and I want you to clearly state the problem you need solved."

Well, that stripped me of my spectator status and added to the almost overwhelming fear that was bubbling inside me. Yet, when I bent over and pressed my forehead to the animal's, everything changed. Suddenly, I no longer felt as if I were being forced to witness death from some impersonal viewpoint. Instead, as my head made union with the animal's head, I sensed its life and energy. I was filled with a combination of sadness and gratitude, with respect and humility, with understanding and acceptance. As I stood back and watched the babalawo begin his sacrificial prayers I was no longer afraid. As his knife slipped effortlessly into the jugular and the animal's blood flowed out,

I could feel the energy and power that only life's blood can provide. Equally important, for the first time in my life, I saw death not as some horrible event to be dreaded and feared but as an integral part of life. Though it would be many years before I experienced knowledge of rebirth, this was the first glimpse that made it possible.

After the ritual, I was neither frightened nor appalled. I was filled with feelings that would take a lot of sorting out, but I knew that the experience was positive.

Whether it was the sacrifice of a rooster or the Paschal Lamb, the kosher slaughter of animals for food or the Crucifixion, authentic religious practice has always included some form of blood sacrifice. In Ifa, we believe in demonstrably improving the lives of those we guide by many means, including blood sacrifice.

FOUR

DEATH AND REBIRTH

K eni hu we gbedegbede
K eni le ju pelepele
K omo eni le n owo gbogbogbo
Le ni sin.

Let us behave gently,
that we may die peacefully;
that our children may stretch out
their hands
upon us in burial.

—OYEKUMEJI

I n Ifa, Death is known as Icu (E-kew), and he is said to claim his victims through the use of a hammerlike instrument. Our history teaches that at first Icu claimed his victims at their preordained time, but sometime in the dimmest past he began to take men, women, and children from the earth capriciously. Most of the orisa were angry, but they were also afraid to interfere. Only Orunmila took action. One day, while Icu was distracted, Orunmila snatched Icu's hammer and hid it away. When Icu discovered that his instrument of death had disappeared, he was furious. He stormed his way to Orunmila's house and demanded that the hammer be returned. Orunmila refused.

"I must have my hammer," Icu shouted.

"No," replied Orunmila, "you were charged by Oludumare to take those whose time has come, and instead you have been taking humans anytime it pleases you."

"If people do not die, the earth will die!" Icu responded.

"You have no right to take people before their time," Orunmila countered.

And so the argument raged on. Indeed, it raged for hundreds or perhaps thousands of years, until finally Orunmila realized the logic in what Icu said. If people never died, the earth would be unable to feed them all. Still, Orunmila was not willing to concede. Finally he summoned the desperate and chastened Icu to his compound.

"Icu," Orunmila began, "I have thought long and hard about returning your hammer. It is true that if humans do not die, the earth must perish. But it is also true that you cannot remove people whenever the mood strikes you. So I have reached a solution. I will return your hammer to you, but with one condition."

"Anything!" Icu shouted.

"Well then," Orunmila replied, "I will return your hammer on the condition that you swear never to take my children before their time."

"I promise!" Icu said, but pausing, he asked, "How will I know your children?"

"They will wear my *ide* (bracelet) on their left wrists."

To this day, Ifa followers wear a two-colored, beaded bracelet, fed and blessed by the babalawo, on their left wrists. In so doing they guarantee that Death, should Icu visit early, will respect his pact with Orunmila and not return until their preordained time.

Many of my godchildren have asked, "Why, when Ifa believes in blood reincarnation, would it be such a tragedy to die before your time?" It's a good question with an important answer.

Ifa teaches that "Earth is the marketplace and Heaven our home."

Aye loja
Orun nile
A difa fun Oludumare, agotun
Oba ataye ma tuu
Bee dele aye
Bee gbagbe orun
Aye loja
Orun nile
E o jiyin
E o jabo
Oun ti e ri
Oyeku-Ogbe.

The world is a marketplace
Ikole Orun is our permanent home.
Cast divination oracle for Oludumare
The perfect organizer of the world.
If you come to the world and forget Ikole Orun
Note that the world is just a marketplace
Whereas Ikole Orun is our permanent home.

In the intricate structure of rebirth, we visit Earth for specific learning and growth experiences, and when they have been achieved, we return "home." To leave before we have attained that particular wisdom and knowledge is disruptive. Premature death interrupts the cycle, both from a time and from a learning perspective, and causes us to metaphorically lose our place in line. It is likely that the Catholic concept of limbo, in which the soul is trapped in a never-never land between Heaven and Hell, is an adaptation of this ancient idea.

To understand the importance of a "proper" death, it is essential to understand the significance of rebirth. In Ifa, we do not believe in reincarnation in the usual sense. Reincarnation implies a number of conditions, including the migration of the soul from one body to another—its destiny determined, in large part, by the life it lived this time around. Reincarnation also includes concepts such as karma, or coming back as a more or a less highly evolved being. One could return as any kind of matter—a toad, a mushroom, or a stone. The teachings of Ifa are significantly different. We believe in rebirth *within* the family. The Yoruba names *Babatunde* (Father returns), *Yetunde* (Mother returns), *Jabatunji* (Father wakes once again), and *Sotunde* (the wise man returns) all offer vivid literal evidence about the Ifa concept of familial or bloodline rebirth.

I remember calling my friend and teacher Afolabi Epega shortly after my father died. After expressing his sorrow at my loss, he jovially stated, "Well, your next child can be Babatunde!" It is this understanding that allows us to feel sorrow at the passing of loved ones along with the joy that, through our children and our children's children, we can provide for their return.

There is no simple guarantee that your grandfather or great uncle will "come back" in the birth of your child, however. Ifa teaches that we all have a "perfect twin" or double. When the time arrives for a spirit to return to Earth through the conception of a new life in the direct blood lineage of the family, one of the component entities returns while the other remains in Heaven. The spirit that returns does so in the form of a guardian Ori. One's guardian Ori, which is represented and contained in the crown of the head, represents not only the spirit and energy of one's previous blood relative but the accumulated wisdom he or she has acquired through a myriad of lifetimes. This is not to be confused with one's spiritual Ori, which contains destiny, but instead refers to the coming back to Earth of one's personal blood Ori through one's new life and experiences.

In Ifa we constantly remind the devotee that "you crown your own head." Too often this is interpreted to mean "you make your own life happen" or "you are responsible for most of what occurs." Although that is true, it means much more. It literally means "the crown of your head, or Ori." Through ancestor worship and offerings you can access or take advantage of the accumulated wisdom that has been given you since conception. Through the act of creating children and the cycle of rebirth, you continue the process, you increase the knowledge, and you provide for the continuation of the flow and for the "crowning" of the next generation. For this, children become the greatest blessing in our lives. The Odu Iworidi addresses this issue specifically:

Kosi abiyamo ti ko lee bi Awo l'omo
Kosi abiyamo ti ko lee be Orunmila.
Baba eni, bioba bi ni ni pipe,
Bopetiti, a tun nbi Baba eni l'omo.
A daa f'Orunmila, ti o wipe:
Oun maa m'Orun bo wa si aye,
Oun maa mu Aye lo s'Orun.
Ki o baa le se bee dandan,
Ifa ni ki o ru ohun-gbogbo ni mejimeji,
Abo ati Ako bayi: Agbo kan, Agutan kan,
Okuko kan, Ewure kan, Akuko-adiye kan,
Agbedo-ayiye kan; ati beebee lo.
O gbo o rubo.
Bee ni aye nbisii ti won si nre sii.

There is no child-bearing woman who cannot give birth to
     an Ifa priest.
There is no child-bearing woman who cannot give birth to
     Orunmila.
Our father, if he gives birth to us in full,
Inevitably we shall in time give birth to him in turn.
Our mother, if she gives birth to us in full,
Inevitably we shall give birth to her in turn.

What this means is that if your father or mother gives birth to you in full, someday you or your children will give birth to them in turn. It is the continuity and glue that provides the Ifa devotee with the ability to live life to its fullest, without fear of death.

Death is only to be feared when it occurs prematurely, especially in unborn or very young children. Their spirits, known as *abiku*, are said to be souls who are seeking to torment their parents. Their early deaths are often followed by another one a year or so later. In order to break the chain of death, the babalawo is usually consulted. A small iron chain, which has been specially prepared by the babalawo, is attached to the left ankle of the child upon birth. This will "hold the child to the earth" and prevent his or her death. My own son, Dashiel, whose half-brother died at nine weeks of age, wore such an anklet. The doctors at the hospital may have thought it strange, but the anklet was placed on his left leg just moments after birth, and the hospital staff was informed not to remove it under any circumstances.

Long life is such a requirement for Ifa devotees that verse after verse of our poetry and prayers refer to it. Indeed, it is said that an individual can be buried only by those younger, and in the distant past *abiku*, or those who died before their time, were given no formal funeral rites. A famous Ifa prayer says, "May I know the blessing of being buried by my son."

So, in Ifa, death is simply the passageway from the marketplace (Earth) to Heaven. Rebirth is the return of the soul as part of the incarnation of a new blood relative. And when a body has grown old and tired, when its destiny has been fulfilled and the wisdom and experience of a lifetime accumulated, then it is time to shed the old body, replenish the spirit, and prepare to return reborn and refreshed.

FIVE

THE DAYS OF THE WEEK

MONDAY *(Ojo Aje)*
Day for Financial Success. Monday belongs to Yemonja/Olukun. A good day to initiate new business ventures. The best day to perform rituals for prosperity or financial success.

TUESDAY *(Ojo Isegun)*
Day of Victory. Tuesday belongs to Ogun. Rituals for overcoming enemies or conflicts are best performed on this day. Also beneficial for business and financial events.

WEDNESDAY *(Ojo Riru)*
Day of Confusion. Wednesday belongs to Oya. A bad day for new undertakings or major projects of any kind. This day, as well as Saturday, is inappropriate for most ritual sacrifices. The famous herbal black soap used to dispel evil is not used on these days out of respect for the *aje* (witches), who are said to hold meetings on Wednesday and Saturday. This is the proper day, however, for rituals to the witches.

THURSDAY *(Ojo Bo)*
Day of Fulfillment. Thursday belongs to Sango. A perfect day for marriage. For the beginning of any long-term project. For digging the foundation for your home. For any long-term goals one needs fulfilled.

FRIDAY *(Ojo Ete)*
Day of Trouble. Friday belongs to Osun. A particularly bad day for travel or moving from one home or business location to another. A good day for chiefs by virtue of their intention to remain in one location for a length of time.

SATURDAY *(Ojo Abameta)*
Day of Evil Resolutions.Saturday belongs to Esu. Like Wednesday, a bad day to undertake major projects and for the use of most charms. Favorable on this day is preparation, as opposed to use, of amulets and protective charms. The second of the "witches' days."

SUNDAY *(Ojo Aiku)*
Day of Long Life and Tranquillity. Sunday belongs to Obatala. The day for settling differences. Useful for long-range planning and the perfect day for preparation of amulets and charms for longevity and good health.

Each day of the week is associated with the qualities of one or more orisa. Offerings to that orisa are best made only on the specified day, and in the chapters that follow, you will be reminded of the days on which to make offerings. This outline should help you understand that specific orisa are chosen for specific outcomes.

HOW THE DAYS CAME TO BE

In the beginning of time, Oludumare (God) called all the orisa together into a sacred garden known as Ogbeise, or the Garden of Command. The garden was ruled by the sixteen sacred odus that form the cornerstone of the sacred texts of Ifa. Their combined powers were so great that whatever wishes the inhabitants made were destined to come to pass. There was one exception: Oludumare decreed that the wishes of the inhabitants *must* be positive in nature. He also informed the visitors that they would have only seven days to spend in the Ogbeise.

Immediately, Esu-Odara (the divine messenger or intermediary between human being and orisa, human and God) prayed for prosperity of all kinds to fill the garden. As Oludumare had promised, the wish was granted, and almost instantly the garden was filled with every conceivable kind of wealth. The inhabitants of the garden decided to share their wealth with those outside and spent the entire day spreading their wealth throughout the world. That night Oludumare inquired as to how they had spent their day. When they related their activities to him, he named the day Ojo Aje, the day of financial success and prosperity. The day was Monday.

The next day Oludumare urged them to continue to pray for beneficial things. But those outside the sacred garden, who had received wealth the day before, rushed inside looking for more treasures. Quarrels ensued, but those properly inside used the power of the sixteen sacred odus to command victory over the invaders. The wish immediately came to pass, and the outsiders were subdued and driven away.

At day's end, when Oludumare reviewed their behavior, he named this day Ojo Isegun, the day of victory. This was Tuesday.

Early on the third day, a powerful wind blew into the sacred garden. The clarity and beauty of the Ogbeise was distorted with dust and dirt; plants and flowers perished. Those inside spent their entire day cleaning and washing, trying to keep their possessions from blowing away. They were so involved with the storm that they forgot to pray, and nothing got organized. When Oludumare came that evening, they told him about the events. Consequently, Oludumare named the day Ojo Riru, the day of confusion. It was Wednesday.

The next day, following the dust storm, those inside prayed for rain and for order to be restored. Their wishes were granted and rain came to feed the new crops and the vegetation that had been destroyed by the dust storm. Life inside the garden returned to normal. All the orisa were happy and continued to pray for all the good things in life. That evening they realized this was the best day they had ever witnessed. When they informed Oludumare of their happiness, he named the day Ojo Asededaye or Ojo Bo, the day of fulfillment. The day was Thursday.

Oludumare then informed them to prepare for a long journey the following morning. Early the next day they all prayed for a safe journey to their destination. The distance they traveled was astronomical and the potential hardships severe, but because they had prayed for a safe journey, they had no problems reaching their destination. On their return, however, it was a different story. Every unforeseen obstacle interfered with their progress. The day was completely ruined as they fought to overcome each difficulty. Indeed, they began to doubt they would ever return to their sacred garden. Finally, they summoned all their powers and were able to fight their way back to the Ogbeise in the dead of night. They all vowed never again to undertake a journey like this on that day again. Due to these events, Oludumare named this day Ojo Ete, day of trouble or turbulence. The day was Friday.

On the sixth day, Oludumare summoned Esu-Odara and informed him that he had decided that Esu-Odara could not control all riches and wealth on Earth. Instead, he himself would regulate their flow and disbursement through sacrifice and ritual. Esu-Odara became angry that responsibility was being taken from him and challenged Oludumare. Esu was thrice defeated. Realizing he alone could not defeat Oludumare, Esu called together all 401 inhabitants of the garden and proposed the following: one, Oludumare would never survive the power of all the orisa pitted against him; two, if he should survive, he would cease to progress in life; three, if he should progress, he could never join them in their lives and works. They all prayed for these events. At the end of the day, Oludumare summoned all 401 orisa together in the Ogbeise. He informed them that their wish could not be granted, because they had violated one of the rules of the sacred garden: they had prayed for evil things to occur, not positive things. Because of this, Oludumare named this day Ojo Abameta, the day of three evil resolutions. The day was Saturday.

On the seventh day, Oludumare came out full of life and power. He began to shower blessings on all the orisa that had opposed him, including Esu-Odara. They were all happy once again and ashamed at their selfish behavior of the previous day. All quarrels were settled, and the order of the orisa was established forevermore. Oludumare named this day Ojo Aiku, the day of longevity. The day was Sunday.

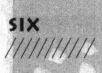

SIX

IN THE BEGINNING. . .

```
|   ||
|   ||
|   ||
||  |
```

—OKANRAN/EGUNTAN
(SACRED ODU THAT SPEAKS
OF CREATION)

ludumare, the single God, assembled all his wealth in one place and sent his messenger out to summon the 401 *irunmoles* (supernatural beings from Heaven, 256 of whom became the sacred odus, or texts, of Ifa). He sent for them so that they could carry his treasures to Earth. They were asked to sacrifice a large lump of pounded yam, a potful of soup, many kola nuts, sheep, pigeon, fowls, and 3,200 cowries and to use the sacrifices to entertain visitors. Oludumare's messenger reached all 401 *irunmoles* and delivered the message, but none of them entertained the messenger with the ordered sacrifices. When the messenger reached Orunmila, he was welcomed heartily and entertained with food. Because of this kindness, the messenger disclosed to Orunmila that he should not be very anxious about carrying the treasures because the most important one was underneath Oludumare's seat.

When the *irunmoles* assembled, they were told of Oludumare's message, and all of them were struggling for what they believed to be the most valuable contents. Some carried money, some food, some other things valuable to them. Oludumare's messenger, talking through his trumpet, told Orunmila to "sit quietly because the most important thing is in the snail's shell." Thus Orunmila sat patiently watching the other *irunmoles* take away all the wealth, property, and various essences they were to carry to Earth.

After they left, Orunmila got up and went straight to where Oludumare sat, took the snail's shell from under his seat, and departed for Earth. Orunmila met the other *irunmoles* at the terminus of the road leading from Heaven to Earth and asked them what was wrong. They responded that the earth was covered with water, and there was no place for them to land. Then Orunmila dipped his hand into the snail's shell and took out a net, which he cast upon the water. He dipped his hand inside the shell a second time and brought out earth, which he cast upon the net. A third time he reached into the shell and brought forth a five-fingered cock and threw him on the net to spread the earth on the net and the water. The cock began to spread said earth, water was moving backward, and the ground was spreading. When it seemed the work was going too slowly, Orunmila himself descended and commanded the small land to be expanded thus: "Be expanded quickly. Be expanded quickly. Be expanded quickly!" He stopped, and the world expanded. There was great joy in Heaven. The place where Orunmila stood, as the first person on Earth, and decreed the world be expanded, is to this day called Ifa-Wara in Ile Ife.

The 401 *irunmoles* descended after Orunmila, who created the land and first tread upon it. He did not allow any of the *irunmoles* to descend onto the land until he had accepted all that they had brought with them and gave to them what he saw fit. They joyfully received their portions.

The *irunmole* were those supernatural beings from Ikole Orun (Heaven) who first visited Ikole Aye (Earth). It was they who made Earth habitable for human beings. They are the energy from which all of nature derives. Orunmila, who made it possible for the *irunmole* to descend to Earth, accepted only 256 of them, including Ogun, god of metals and creativity; Obatala, god of creation; Sango, god of thunder; Osun, river goddess; Ososi, god of hunting; Esu, god of justice; Osonyin, god of medicine; and, most intelligent of all, reverently called god of intelligence or knowledge, Orunmila.

These *irunmole* were not born of Earth, nor would they die here. They were the link between human beings and Oludumare (God) at the creation of the earth, and they are the only link now. Individually and collectively they serve as the medium through which Oludumare imparts to humankind his scientific knowledge of nature in general and his esoteric knowledge of words, known as Ifa.

Once they had brought Oludumare's treasures to Earth, the *irunmole* ascended to Ikole Orun (Heaven) and did not return. Because they had acted as mentors and teachers, their departure left a gap or void between human beings and Oludumare. How could human beings continue to communicate with God? The logical answer was that the spirits or energy of the *irunmole* would be invoked to carry messages. From that time until now, the *irunmole* are the only clear path to Oludumare, to communication with him.

Everything considered, it seemed logical for human beings to invoke the spirits of the *irunmole* through the medium of the objects most cherished by them during their tenure on Earth. These included their tools, their images, or the media by which they had descended to Ikole Aye or ascended back to Ikole Orun, such as the *ope* Ifa, or sacred palm tree, which is used extensively by Orunmila as well as others.

There are many other examples:

Ogun, sent by Oludumare to teach humans blacksmithing and metallurgy, is usually summoned esoterically by using iron objects or the *mariwo* (palm frond) as objects of invocation.

Orunmila, also known as Ela (the Pure) and the only *irunmole* to have brought down the wisdom of Oludumare through the teachings of Ifa, is invoked through the *ikin* Ifa, or sacred fortified palm kernel, from the sacred palm tree *ope* Ifa.

Sango, orisa of thunder, is invoked with the *ose* (double-headed ax), *edun ara* (thunderstone/celt), *orogbo* (bitter kola nut), *epo* (red palm oil), and others. The double-headed ax was Sango's symbol of office during his time on Earth; thunderstones are created when lightning strikes rocks; bitter kola was one of his favorite foods; red palm oil was a medicinal antidote for his annoyance.

Esu, orisa of *asé* and opportunity, was the alias of Esu-Odara, Ola-ilu, Elegba, and Oriki Oko, among others. He was the town savior, who moved about with a stone. Today the *yangi,* or sacred stone that represents Esu, is used to call his spirit.

Obatala or Oosanla, orisa of creation, is invoked with *ofun* (chalk), lead, or a small metal bell.

Osun, orisa of sweet waters, is invoked through a clay pot or vessel filled with sacred stones from the river.

Osonyin, orisa of herbs and medicine, has *ere* (his image) as well as the *mariwo* (palm frond) for calling his spirit.

To this day, the orisa are invoked through these same sacred objects. Invocation is a powerful tool for positive change, and as you learn about the major orisa in the chapters to come, it will become clear why certain orisa are called for specific problems and how this came to be.

PART TWO

THE WAY OF THE ORISA

ORUNMILA

ORUNMILA! Eleri Ipin,
   Ibikeji Oludumare,
      A-je-ju-Oogun,
   Obiriti, A-p'ijo-iku-da
Oluwa mi, A-to-i-ba-j'aye
   Oro a-bi-ku-j'igbo
   Oluwa mi, Ajiki,
   Ogege a-gb' aye-gun;
Odudu ti ndub ori emere;
A-tun-ori-ti-ko sunwon se
      A-mo-i-ku.
   Olowa Aiyere,
   Agiri Ile-llogbon;
Oluwa mi; amoimotan,
   A ko mo O tan kose
   A ba mo tan iba se ke.

Orunmila! Witness of fate,
Second to Oludumare [God];
Thou are far more efficacious than
   medicine,
Thou the Immense Orbit that averts the
   day of Death.
My Lord, Almighty to save,
Mysterious Spirit that fought death.
To Thee salutation is first due in the
   morning,
Thou Equilibrium that adjusts World
   Forces,
Thou art the One whose exertion it is to
reconstruct the creature of bad lot;
Repairer of ill-luck,
He who knows thee becomes immortal.
Lord, the undeposable king,
Perfect in the House of Wisdom!
My Lord! Infinite in knowledge!
For not knowing thee in full, we are futile,
Oh, if we could but know thee in full,
all would be well with us.

—MORNING PRAYER OF THE BABALAWO

SEVEN

ORUNMILA

EBOS FOR ORUNMILA Offerings to Orunmila are made only at the direction and under the supervision of the babalawo.

Among the orisa, the word of Orunmila, as expressed through his priests, is absolute, equivalent to the Christian belief in Holy Scripture. In the Ifa tradition, it is unthinkable to embark upon any major task without first consulting Orunmila to ascertain whether or not the proposed action is wise and to glean its probable outcome. Only the extremely foolhardy would go ahead with anything as serious as marriage, a new business venture, the conception of a child, or treatment of a mental or physical illness without seeking the guidance of Orunmila through the babalawo.

Ifa teaches that Orunmila was attendant at the act of creation along with Oludumare (God). Because of this, Orunmila was also the witness of fate and knows the likelihood of all future events. It is said that he lived on Earth for many years but that one day, tired and disappointed with the behavior of humans, he returned to Heaven and vowed never again to return to Earth. Catastrophe followed, as humans had no way to identify the correct course for future actions or to repair the problems created by past mistakes.

Once more, Orunmila returned. Once more, those who followed his teachings and performed the proper sacrifices prospered. Many, however, did not. Again, Orunmila left Earth for Heaven. This time, however, so that he would not have to return, he left behind his spiritual self in the form of the sacred palm nuts used by his priests. Through divination, babalawos are both literally and figuratively in touch with Orunmila and can access his knowledge of future events. Not only can the babalawo forecast the likely outcome of the event, but, through communication with Orunmila, he can prescribe the sacrifices necessary to assure a favorable outcome.

Priests of Orunmila must undergo years of training and elaborate initiations. They must memorize literally thousands of odus—each of which represents a specific tale or myth—and demonstrate their understanding of them. When the babalawo casts the *opele* (the chain of halfseed shells) or "pounds the nuts" (uses the *ikin* for divination), he is asking Orunmila to indicate which particular odu, and hence which tales and information, are most applicable to the client's situation or problem. Carl Jung would have called it "synchronicity," meaning that the client and the specific odu were meant to come together at that particular moment. It is neither chance nor accident.

Many of the sacred odus help explain the role of Orunmila as diviner, healer, and instrument for change.

He is prophet:

Orunmila prophesied, it came to pass.
It came to pass Bara, Agbonniregun.
They asked what it was that was coming to pass.
He answered that it was the blessing of wealth foretold.

He is maker of miracles:

When our own handicraft suffices us
Reliance is never placed on theft;
Theft can never suffice us, except our own honorable labor:
This declares the Oracle to Orunmila
When he set out from township to rural areas.
He was warned that he would do marvelous acts of kindness,
But that he would be repaid evil for good;
But the Almighty God would requite him manifold.
And all the deities would also repay him amply.

He saw a lame man, and he restored his limbs;
The lame man failed to express any gratitude.
Orunmila called him back
And asked why he failed to be grateful.
He saw an albino, touched his skin;
The albino'-s skin became restored to normalcy.
He saw a hunchbacked man, and touched his hunch;
The hunch on his back dropped to the ground.
He called back the man and asked why he was ungrateful.
He found a woman laboring of child;
He took care of her, and she was delivered safely.
He met people where somebody had died of an illness;
The deceased, borne in a coffin, was about to be buried.
Orunmila stopped the concourse of mourners and raised the dead
    to life.
They all acclaimed Orunmila, saying, "All hail to His Majesty!"
Orunmila got to another place,
There Death was intimidating someone,
Orunmila began to sing as a challenge:
"If I see Death I would crush him in a fight."
If I catch sight of Plague I would best him in combat;
Woroji, woroji, wo!
Death fled away in fear of Orunmila;
Plague took flight to avoid Orunmila.

He is a doctor:

Ela (another name for Orunmila) looses it, Ela binds it
Declared oracle for Orunmila,
Saying that the patients he treats
Will all receive complete cure.

He is a savior:

Ela Wori it is who saves the world from ruin:
When the world of Obalufe became confused,
Ela Wori it was who restored order into it;
When the taboo breakers of Akila spoiled the town,
Ela Iwori it was who put things right for the people.
When day turned into night in the town of Okerekese, and the
     sages of the town were baffled,
Ela Iwori it was who came to the aid of Oluyori, its king, with a
     remedy:
Whenever Elegbara plans to turn the world upside down,
Ela Iwori it is who obstructs him;
Ela Iwori receives no money,
Ela Iwori receives no kola nuts,
Yet it is he who rectifies unhappy destinies.

Here is an example of a divination and how the babalawo would use
it. A woman, unable to bear children, comes to a babalawo for divination. He casts. The odu is called Iworidi.

```
I    II
II   I
II   I
I    II
```

This is what it says:

Kosi Abiyamo ti ko lee bi Awo l'omo Kosi Abiyamo ti ko Iee bi Orun-
mila. Baba eni, bioba bi'ni ni pipe, Bopetiti, a tun nbi Baba eni l'omo'
Yeye eni, bioba bi'ni ni pipe, Bopetiti, a tun nbi Yeye eni l'omo. A daa
f'Orunmila, ti o wipe: Oun maa m'Orun bo wa si aye, Oun maa mu Aye lo
s'Orun. Ki o baa le se bee dandan, Ifa ni ki o ru ohun-gbogbo ni mejmeji,
Abo ati aka bayi: Agbo kan, Agutan kan, Obujo kan, Ewure kan, Akuko-
adiye kan, Agbebo-adiye kan; ati beebee lo. O gbo o rubo. Bee ni aye nbisii
ti won si nre sii.

There is no child-bearing woman who cannot give birth to an Ifa priest. There is no child-bearing woman who cannot give birth to Orunmila. Our father, if he gives birth to us in full, inevitably we shall in time give birth to him in turn. Our mother, if she gives birth to us in full, inevitably we shall in turn give birth to her in turn.

Ifa was consulted for Orunmila, when he said: I will bring Heaven down to Earth. I will take Earth up to heaven.

So that he might successfully accomplish his task, he was told to offer everything in twos, one male and one female.

Thus: one ram and one lamb; one he goat and one she goat; one cock and one hen; and so on. Orunmila listened, heeded, obeyed, and sacrificed.

Thus the earth became fruitful and multiplied greatly.

The odu refers to the client's problem. It states that she can have children. The babalawo will then cast again to find the specific sacrifice necessary to accomplish this.

Divination will specify which orisa must be placated, what to sacrifice/offer, and what changes the client must make. But only through consultation with Orunmila is the babalawo able to identify and offer solutions. Orunmila can provide help for virtually every human problem.

Each of the following seven chapters begins with a list of the qualities of the "children" of that particular orisa. These lists should give you a good starting point for identifying your own personal guardian spirit. (Only through divination by a babalawo can your guardian orisa be absolutely determined.) I will then recommend appropriate offerings and the best day of the week on which to make them. May you find in the orisa examples of the strength and wisdom you'll need to pursue your life path.

ELEGBARA/ESU

Akakanika li aa pe Ifa,
   Akakinika le aape Odu.
Alapasapa-i jaka lu liaape Esu
   Odara,
Eye kan fo feerefe-o-wole li
   aape aje-
omo Olukun-son-de Oba Olubo-
   omi, Ogo Owoni.
Esu-Odara, iwo liote ilu di yi do.
Iwo nikiijeki ebi kiopa
   Onisegun ilu;
Iwo nikiijeki ebi ilu yi ree, Emi
   Adahunse
ilu yi ree, Esu-Odara majekebi pa
   mi atee beebee.
Ewe Ifa naa: Ewo Abomoda kan,
   ebu (erupe agbede) aro,
efun ati osun. Ao te Odu Osetura
   lori erupe-agbede
tiabuwale, ao sa Igede tiowa loka
   yi bi a ti pee
sibiyi sori erupe (ebu) naa,
   kiadaa pomo efun
li owo otun lati fi te odu Ose,
   kiadaapomo osun
li owo osi pelu erupa naa lati fi te
   Odu Otura
si ara ewe Abamoda naa. Kiapa
   Obi alawe merin

tiodara fun Ifa yi. Owu dudu ati
   funfun niki a
papo fi sooro soke ninu ile. Eyo
   ataa re meje ate
awe Obi kan niki a maa je fi fun
   un nibiti
a sooro si. Ao maa fisa Igede naa
   biatipee nibiyi
lojo o jumo.

Akakanika is the name given to
Ifa; Alakakanika is the name
given to odu. Alapasappa-ijaka Iu
is the name given to Esu-Odara.
Esu-Odara thou established this
town. Thou delivered the babalawos of the town from being
starved. Thou delivered the
physicians of the town from being
starved as well as the herbalists.
I am the babalawo of the town. I
am the physician of the town. I
am the herbalist of the town;
don't let me be starved. Don't let
me be without wealth or wives or
many children.

—OSETURA

ELEGBARA/ESU

CHILDREN OF ESU WILL ENJOY

- ▲ sex
- ▲ having fun
- ▲ large groups of people and parties
- ▲ travel
- ▲ good food
- ▲ wine or liquor
- ▲ cigarettes or cigars
- ▲ dancing
- ▲ brightly colored clothes
- ▲ costumes
- ▲ many friendships within their own gender
- ▲ communications
- ▲ movies and theater

YOU WILL HAVE TROUBLE

- ▲ functioning in confined environments
- ▲ being monogamous
- ▲ taking orders
- ▲ working within a large corporate atmosphere
- ▲ being on time
- ▲ being structured
- ▲ dieting
- ▲ quitting smoking or drinking
- ▲ sticking to a formal exercise program
- ▲ being bored

YOU WILL HAVE A HIGHLY DEVELOPED SENSE OF

- ▲ right and wrong
- ▲ humor
- ▲ practical jokes
- ▲ getting even
- ▲ sensuality

EBOS FOR ESU   As one of the pantheon of Ifa warrior orisa, Esu enjoys highly spiced foods. Chili peppers, peppercorns, and jalapeños are all suitable offerings to Esu. A strong cigar, rum, gin, or beer are highly favored by him as well. Red palm oil—a staple of all orisa with the exception of Obatala—is often poured on Esu or in front of his image. Pigeon, rooster, and male goat are all offered to Esu. Many devotees begin each day by sprinkling cool water on or in front of Esu as a way of "cooling" his temper and asking for pleasantness in their own day. This is my own daily prayer to Esu, recited while I am in the process of making the offering:

> *Esu, please open my paths and doors and roads*
> *and the paths and doors and roads of those I love.*
> *And please close the paths and doors and roads of*
> *those who would do me, or those I love, harm.*

Esu's day is Saturday.

EIGHT

Esu (pronounced A-shew) is the most misunderstood of the orisa. He is also one of the most powerful. Esu rules through the *ajogun,* the beneficial as well as detrimental forces of the universe. These forces were divinely endowed by Oludumare to be either good and generous or bad and evil. The good *ajogun* control wealth, children, wives/husbands, success, love, and so on. The evil *ajogun* control death, illness, loss, mental unrest, and similar forces. Esu has all the *ajogun* at his command and can be kind and generous if approached positively or can unleash the demonic forces of the evil *ajogun* when provoked. With this ability, Esu serves a dual purpose, both good and bad, in human existence. Esu, through sacrifice, serves as messenger between humans and the other orisa and between humans and God.

> *Bi a ba rubo, ki a mu t Esu Kuro.*
> Whatever sacrifice is offered, a portion belongs to Esu.

Nothing can go forward without his help. He comes first in all ceremonies and must receive part of all offerings. An Ifa priest will chant:

> The world is broken into pieces;
> The world is split wide open,
> The world is broken without anyone to mend it;
> The world is split open without anybody to sew it.
> Cast Ifa for the six elders
> Who were coming down from Ile Ife.
> They were asked to take care of Mole.

They were told they would do well

If they made sacrifice.

If the sacrifice to Esu is not made,

It will not be acceptable in heaven.

OSE MEJI

The importance of Esu is clear, yet the first Christian missionaries were convinced that Esu was the Devil. These missionaries confused Esu's ability to trick and punish those who do not sacrifice with an innate predisposition to do so. Esu does punish, but he does not punish capriciously. Esu rewards, but he does not reward the undeserving. His apparent contradictions are not contradictory at all. Rather, they are logical responses to the behavior of those he deals with. From a Christian viewpoint of divine forgiveness, the actions of Esu toward those who ignore their obligations might indeed seem extremely harsh and unforgiving, the work of "a devil." Yet, in the Yoruba cosmology— in which the universe contains all possibilities, both good and bad, and individuals have opportunities for controlling their own destinies by working with natural forces—the failure to control one's own destiny is seen as an act of gross stupidity with potentially dire consequences. Esu is in charge of those consequences!

To those who work with and not against the natural order of the universe, who "sacrifice" in both the literal and the philosophical meaning of the word, the potential is unlimited and the rewards beyond comprehension. Esu is in charge of these as well! As in all things in Ifa, the individual "crowns his own head." The decision to wear a crown or a dunce cap is a personal matter, and Esu awaits your decision. Devotees of Esu often refer to him as "Baba" or Father. They are known as Esubiyi (son of Esu) or Esugbayi (one claimed by Esu).

Esu's own cap is often the subject of his mythology. A famous Yoruba story centers around two farmers, both neighbors and friends, who had failed to sacrifice. Esu, in his tricolored hat, one-third red, one-third white, and one-third blue, walked down a road between the two offending farmers.

"Did you notice the fellow in the red hat?" the first farmer asked.

"No," replied his friend and neighbor, "there was a fellow who passed this way, but his hat was blue and white."

"You're wrong," insisted the first.

"No, you're being insulting," retorted the second.

And soon, the insults increased, and a physical fight began. The two were dragged before the local *oba,* where each told his story. As the *oba* was ready to sentence them for fighting, Esu suddenly appeared

Onagbara Esu mask, worn on top of the worshiper's head, c. 1950.

and explained that it was he who had caused their problems, because they had not sacrificed. The lesson, hopefully, was learned.

Esu's ability to appear instantly is one of his many magical attributes. He travels instantly anywhere and everywhere in the world, and it is his speed that carries the sacrifice to Oludumare, that enables your paths and doors to open quickly when you need them.

Logemo orun; A-nla-ka lu; Papa-wara; A-tuka-ma-se-sa

The indulgent child of Heaven; he whose greatness is everywhere manifested; the hurrying, sudden one; he who breaks in fragments and cannot be gathered together!

Esu is also the possessor of divine *asé,* the inner energy and power that allows us to access the right side of the brain and use its powers. *Asé* is similar to, but more than, aura, soul, or spirituality. It is a living, breathing, palpable flow of energy that can either increase or diminish, depending upon our behavior.

It is believed that after Oludumare created such evil things as death, disease, illness, pestilence, plague, temper, jealousy, fighting, and loss, and after he created such blessings as love, wives, husbands, children, money, and long life, he created Esu's powers. Esu's powers allowed him to control or limit the excesses of evil, whose powers would otherwise have been unlimited. By controlling the powers of evil through sacrifice, Esu makes available to the men and women who dwell on Earth the blessings of the good things and the orisa that symbolize them.

This is in no way meant to suggest that Esu is some solemn dispenser of justice. Indeed, that would be as far as possible from the truth and totally at odds with the Yoruba paradigm of life. Zorba the Greek could well have been Yoruba, for Yorubas believe that life is meant to be enjoyed. It is the enjoyment of life that Esu symbolizes, and he himself enjoys every minute of every day.

He loves music and dance costumes and laughter. He loves good food and wine. Moderation is a characteristic of other orisa, not Esu. He wants what he wants, and he wants it now. He is rampantly sexual, and every male Esu figure contains either an upward spike of hair or a spike of iron to symbolize his constant phallic capacities. Though

Pair of Esu figures, Imodi, Nigeria. The male figure is Esu as hunter. The female has medicine bottles for a hairdo.

usually symbolized as a male figure, the actual Esu shrines in Nigeria consist of both male and female Esu. The male figure will generally clasp swords, spears, or fly whisk (symbols of magical power); the female will clasp her large, milk-filled breasts. Esu, like all orisa in the Yoruba pantheon, contains both male and female characteristics—just as all humans contain both.

Esu can never be bored. He will easily and willingly provoke conflict or mischief among others simply to get some action going. He uses trickery and illusion to both punish and reward. He is a master of herbal magic and medicine.

When an individual receives his Esu, it carries with it certain responsibilities. Each Saturday, Esu must be fed. Gin or rum should be spat upon his face; in this way, your *asé*—a gift from Esu and contained, in part, in your saliva—will combine with the liquor he receives. Red palm oil should be rubbed into his surface or poured in front of his figure, toasted corn or grains can be given in a dish, and a white candle will be lighted for him. Then you may ask of Esu, "Open my paths and doors and roads and the paths and doors and roads of those I love. And close the paths and doors and roads of those who would do me or those I love harm." This simple prayer covers a multitude of possibilities, yet should not prevent you from asking for specific problems to be solved or desires to be fulfilled.

Remember, Esu is not a toy or game. He is a real and powerful energy source. Be careful of what you ask. As the old Chinese wisdom goes, "To destroy your enemy, grant him his wishes!" Though in Ifa we believe that our wishes are more likely to be rational and not destructive if we are integrated and fully aware of ourselves in relation to the universe, it is equally clear that we should be careful not to act capriciously.

One of the famous stories regarding Esu is how the trickster can occasionally be tricked. A devotee went to his Esu and began rubbing palm kernel oil on the figure. Now, in the mythology of Ifa, palm kernel oil is something that Esu simply hates! While rubbing the oil onto the figure, the man said, "Esu, I know you hate this substance, and if it were up to me, I would never give it to you, but so-and-so insisted I give it to you." Having placed the forces in action, he was depending upon Esu to visit his wrath upon the man who supposedly instructed him to give Esu the offending substance. Once Esu had accomplished his task, the individual would quickly clean the palm kernel oil off Esu, replacing it with red palm oil to soothe and placate the orisa. Personally I wouldn't try to outwit Esu. Too smart can be dumb.

Esu slept in the house
But the house was too small for him.
Esu slept on the verandah
But the verandah was too small for him.
Esu slept in a nut
At last he could stretch himself.
Esu walked through a groundnut farm.
The tuft of his hair was just visible.
If it had not been for his huge size,
He would not have been visible at all.
Having thrown a stone yesterday,
He kills a bird today.
Lying down, his head hits the roof.
Standing up, he cannot look into the cooking pot.
Esu turns right into wrong,
wrong into right.

YORUBA PRAYER

Huge and small, tall and short, active and inactive—just a few of the seemingly contradictory facets of this powerful orisa. But in the greater sense, there are no contradictions at all, for Esu represents choices—your choices. That you see them as limited is simply your perception; Esu knows that limitlessness really exists. You, as this handsome prince of the Yoruba pantheon, can be big or small, good or bad, caring or cruel, generous or selfish, loving or self-absorbed. He, unlike the Christian notion of the Devil, does not tempt you or encourage you to make the wrong choices. Rather, he rewards you for making the right ones. When you, of your own volition, choose the wrong course of action, he uses these same actions to punish and point out your foolishness. Cruel? No, simply real. If we cut down the trees of ancient forests, pollute our waters, and poison our air, the results will be as harsh and definitive as any that Esu could conceive. Neither he, nor the universe we are part of, "forgives." If we survive our mistakes, we learn from them. If we place dunce caps on our heads, we must remove them. If we sacrifice, we prosper and survive.

That is Esu's role. Though carefree, fun-loving, and loath to be "tied down," his sense of justice is greater than any orisa other than Obatala and Ogun. And his free-wheeling life-style and love of merriment are not contradictions to that sense of justice any more than are any of his other actions. Rather, they are the examples that will hopefully erase our ingrained sense of foreboding, impotence, and helplessness about life and our role in it. Esu says, "Life can be fun, rewarding, and exciting if you make the right choices." How sad that most of us were raised to think that the "right" choices preclude personal enjoyment and satisfaction!

As messenger between God and human, that may be Esu's most important message.

OGUN

Ogun meje l Ogun mi:
Ogun Alara ni gb aja;
Ogun Onire a gb agbo;
Ogun Ikola a gba gbin;
T Elemona ni gb esun-su.
Ogun Akirin a gba iwo agbo;
Ogun gbena-gbena eran ahun l o
ma je.
Ogun Makinde ti Ogun l ehin odi-
Bi on ko ba gba Tapa a go Aboki.
A gba Uku-uku, a gba Kemberi.

There are seven Ogun who belong
    to me:
Ogun of Alara it is who takes dog;
Ogun of Onire always takes ram;
Ogun of the knife [surgery] takes
    snail;
That of Elemona it is who takes
    roasted yam.
Ogun of Akirin takes ram's horn;
Ogun of the artisans eats the
    flesh of tortoise.
Ogun of Makinde, which is Ogun
    outside the compound walls—
He either takes a Tapa or takes
    an Aboki,
Or takes an *uku-uku*, or takes a
    kemberi.

Ogun on ile owo, olona ola, on il
    kangun-kangun ti mbe l orun.

Ogun, the owner of the house of
money, the owner of the house of
riches, the owner of innumerable
houses of heaven.

Orisa ti o wipe t Ogun ko to nkan
    a f owo je su e n igba aimoye.

Whichever divinity regards Ogun
without respect will eat his yams
with his hands [without a knife].
    Four is Ogun's number.
    Palm frond [mariwo] is used to
invoke him.
    Dog is his special friend and
companion.

Ogun has old age.
He has longevity,
He has immortality.
He has noncorruption,
He has time of blessings,
He gives them to you.

—BLESSING FROM AN OGUN
PRIEST

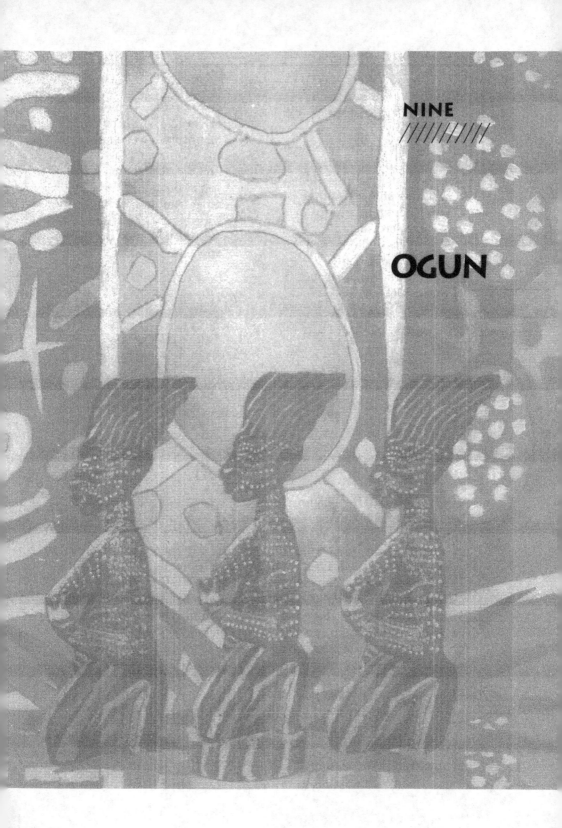

Ogun could be your guardian orisa if you

- ▲ have a profound sense of right and wrong
- ▲ are quick to take offense
- ▲ enjoy physical things
- ▲ prefer small groups to large crowds
- ▲ prefer to "do" rather than talk about doing
- ▲ tend toward a strong physique
- ▲ are attracted to metals
- ▲ prefer the woods or mountains to the sea or the countryside
- ▲ find that others expect you to do things for them
- ▲ have trouble sharing your personal feelings
- ▲ get fuzzy-headed over the opposite sex

EBOS FOR OGUN Ogun, a warrior orisa, likes all things hot and spicy. Peppers in any form, highly spiced foods, 151-proof rum, gin or vodka, black or dark cigars, red palm oil, and, once in a while, honey are all suitable offerings. Rooster and male goat are also offered. Because he is the orisa of metal, there are two particular ebos that refer to his domain. In the event of surgery, buy six different kinds of beans. Soak them overnight, and the next day fry them in palm oil with plenty of pepper, cayenne, and Tabasco sauce. You may include onions and garlic as well. Place this on a plate and offer it to Ogun for a successful outcome to the surgical procedure. If you are buying a new car, or attempting to sell one, purchase an inexpensive cut of meat at the supermarket. Take the raw meat and rub it on all four tires of the automobile while asking Ogun for his protection and blessings. Leave the meat by a railroad track.

Ogun's day is Tuesday.

OGUN

//////////

 gun is a difficult orisa energy for Westerners. We are not comfortable with him. This is particularly true for women.

For example, one of the most famous tales of Ogun tells of a time when he was walking through the woods and came upon a group of his godchildren or followers sitting in a circle. They had obviously been partaking heartily from the many palm wine bottles that dotted the landscape. Ogun, hot and weary from his journey, looked down at the men and asked for a drink. The men only giggled. Instantly, Ogun drew his sword and beheaded each and every one of them. It is this white-hot anger at real or imagined injustice that is most difficult for Westerners to understand and control. Having satisfied his anger, he reached down for a bottle of wine, only to find it empty. Bottle after bottle provided the same results. Ogun realized that the men had not been rude but simply had nothing to offer, and in the contrition of the moment, Ogun threw himself upon his sword and rose to Heaven. From this moment forward, all followers of Ogun, as well as many other orisa worshipers, are careful to lay a bottle on its side once it is empty so that no confusion or harm will befall them.

Another story of Ogun takes place in the Yoruba town of Ire Ekiti. During their Oriki Festival, the townspeople enjoy their food and palm wine in absolute silence, as verbal communication is not allowed. Ogun, returning from his exploits as a warrior, becomes lost in the forest and stumbles upon the Oriki gathering. Thirsty and tired, he looks for hospitality from the group. All he is greeted with is silence and a certain hostile stare. This infuriates Ogun, and he kills the innocents. A passerby enlightens him as to his whereabouts and about the silence of the Oriki Festival. He realizes he has slaughtered his own people. Overcome with remorse, Ogun falls upon his sword and is received into the earth.

It is this precipitous behavior that disturbs most educated people. We are raised, for the most part, to be polite, well behaved, and considerate. And the higher our economic and educational status, the more ingrained is this behavior. As a result of years of being scolded, disciplined, or put down for "reacting," many children of Ogun learned to repress their primary energy source to the point that they are sometimes confused, on the surface at least, with children of Obatala or Yemonja. This repression tends to have the most damaging effect on women, and it can even be extremely dangerous.

Years ago, a lovely young girl was brought to me by her mother. Her readings contained several references to male orisa warrior energy. Her problem, as it turned out, was that she had physically attacked another girl and had hurt her quite badly. The fact that the two had been competing for the same young man only slightly mitigated what had become an involved legal ordeal for the young girl as her former friend's parents pressed charges. As it turned out, there were similar occurrences in her past.

Here was a beautiful teenager who had, through social pressure and parental and societal expectations, learned to repress her instinctive responses. So instead of getting angry or speaking out early on, she repressed her instinctive orisa reactions until, on occasion, they simply exploded in the kind of inappropriate behavior that brought her to me for help.

The children of Ogun must not repress. Though it is not appropriate to lop off the head of someone who cuts you off in traffic or makes a pass at your spouse, it is essential that you do something to get it off your chest when you feel it.

Children of Ogun must understand the totality of their energy and not just its explosive side. To do this you must first examine the odu that brought Ogun into the world, Ogundameji.

Alagbara ni napkun Ade li o difa fi'Ogun, a miki o ru.

Agada, akuko-adiye ati esun-isu. Ifa mi: Agada ye ni

Ogun maafise ise Oro, kiomaa muu Iowo kaakiri, a ni ki

o je esun-isu naa, o jee, orungbe si ngbee, o lo si odo lo mu omi, bi o ti
mu mi tan, o ri awon meji kanti nji nitori eja kan ti wonpa, Ogun niki
awon mejinaa nu suuru ki won lo pin oja naa ni ile, won ko, eki ni so pe
Iwonran ni oun ti wa, ekeji si so pe ni Iwald ni oun ti wa, lehin gbogbo
eyiti won so fun un, o fiada tiowa ni owo re da eja naa si meji fun won,
Ekinni dupe lowo re. O ni: Oun nfe kiofi agada owo re yi laona wa de ilu
oun, O ni oun a soo di Olono, o ni owono yoo te opolopo inkan ti oju ko
niifi pon on kiotoo de odo oun. Enikeji tun dupe, o bee ki o masai la ona
wa da ilu oun bakanna. Ogun ni oun gop. Nje ojo ti—Ogun ti da eja si
meji fun awon meji ti nja li a tinpe ni

Alagbara ni nsokun Ade divines for Ogun. He was advised to sacrifice a cutlass, a cock, and a roasted yam. He was told that he must always go about with his sword because that was his fortune. He was told to eat roasted yam. He did so. He was thirsty after this and went to the river to drink water. As he finished drinking, he saw two figures fighting over a fish they had caught. He advised them to be patient and to go home and share the fish. They ignored him. The first man told him he came from the East and the second from the West, at which point Ogun took his sword and cut the fish in two. The first thanked him and requested that he cut open a footpath from where they were to his town and said that he would enrich Ogun's life if he did. He further said that Ogun would receive valuable things that would give him confidence. The other man also thanked him and made the same request. Ogun agreed, and he has been known as Ogundameji since the day he cut the fish into two.

Properly used, this sense of justice and strength can lead to beneficial results and rewards. Ogun's forcing of the compromise on the men by cutting the fish in two is a good example of this and confirms his divination, which had indicated that his sword would enrich him.

Ogun, the orisa of iron and metals, is a fierce warrior of brute strength, a loner by nature. No orisa man has ever gone to battle without invoking the powers and protection of this mighty warrior. Yet the odu that incarnates Ogun into this world is not an example of his

Mask of Ogun in his hunter aspect, worn on top of the worshiper's head, southwest Nigeria, c. 1950.

tremendous potential for physical action on every level but a call for compromise—an example of the diplomat, not the impetuous primal force.

This is an essential lesson for the children of Ogun. In the mythology of the syncretized versions of Ifa, too often the Ogun archetype is depicted as an almost brutish lout, taking wine, women, and war as his daily fare. Portraying him as the diplomat is meant in no way to diminish the raw power of this orisa of metals.

Ogun has many facets and aspects. He is the father of iron, and, as such, in ancient times his children could be classified into three major categories: warriors, hunters, and farmers. Each was dependent upon the orisa of metal for success in his trade. Still today, knives, spears, arrows, and hoes are among the implements that represent Ogun.

But let me emphasize again that Ogun is not only the orisa of metal, he is the creator with it, and his creative energy is as powerful as his warrior self. Ogun is also concerned with ethics and justice. In Nigeria, for untold years, oaths have been taken by swearing on a piece of metal representing Ogun. Even through the British occupation, the British courts would accept this form of oath within their courts.

Ogun's nature is both vital and violent. His creativity can take the form of teacher, mediator, inventor, or counselor. It can also take the form of warrior, accident, or calamity. It is often in the process of breaking down that new things can be created.

Ogun is, by nature, an extremely hard worker. It is his ability to work almost ceaselessly and with little rest that allowed him to create civilization. This was, in part, the task he was assigned by Oludumare. Yet, as with all orisa qualities, there is an up side and a down side. For Ogun and his children, the down side is that their work is never done. For the children of Ogun, there will be no retirement to sandy beaches; instead, there will always be something more to do. For some of us this would prove an unbearable burden, but for children of Ogun, it is simply the way things are. Work is what they both enjoy and do best, and pleasures are taken intensely and quickly.

The thing that is the most difficult for Ogun's children to come to grips with also comes from Ogundameji, the odu that brought Ogun to Earth.

Okelegbongbo—as'ofun-kilo li o difa f'Ogun, won ni: biobarubo, a ko niigbo iku re laelae, gbogbo aye li o miamaa bee pe: kiobawon tun iwa won se, sugbon kosi eni kan ninu won ti yoo baa duro ro ti ara re. Agbo merin, ewure merin ati igba ademu merin ni ebo, won ru ebo naa Olofin lo ri ebo naa si igun merin aye.

Okalegbongoas ofun-kiio divined for Ogun. He was advised to sacrifice four rams and four large covered calabash so that he might not die, that the whole world would always request him to pave the way for them, but no one would share the sorrow with him in his life.

Children of Ogun, perhaps because of their solitary nature, will tend to hold their emotional pain inside them. This is not to be mistaken for anger, which, as I have clearly pointed out earlier, is easily expressed by the great warrior orisa. It is emotions like sorrow, loss, or disappointment that Oguns tend to hide or deny, and perhaps that is why their sorrows will seldom be understood or shared by others.

Children of Ogun often carry a single chain link in their pockets, for, as Ogundameji states, "A single chain link does not break." I believe this relates as much to the emotional pressures Oguns will have to bear alone as to any physical threat. Ogun, without help, is more than able to handle the physical universe. If you are a child of Ogun, you would be well advised to keep the single link with you at all times.

Oguns are also highly sexual and would tend to have more than the average number of children. If there is one Ogun weakness, it would have to be the opposite sex. Oguns, who are normally clearheaded and determined, will find their resolve melting away over a member of the opposite sex.

A famous Ogun tale explains how Ogun had tired of everyone's constant demands and left civilization for the forest. Without his tools and metals, civilization came to a halt. All the other orisa pleaded with him to return . . . to no avail. Finally Osun, the orisa of sexual love and money, took her five scarves and pot of honey and went near to where Ogun was hiding. She did not call to him or look at or for him. Instead, she began a sensuous dance with her scarves while occasionally dipping into her honey pot and placing the nectar on her shiny lips. Ogun was transfixed. Slowly he crept from his hiding place, virtually hypnotized by the beauty and sensuality of this beautiful orisa. Osun pretended not to notice him and continued her dance. Closer and closer he crept, until he was just inches away from this alluring creature. It was then that Osun reached into her honey pot and spread the honey on Ogun's lips. It was too much even for this warrior orisa. Ogun, forgetting his determination, followed Osun back to civilization, and life for the people of Earth could once again progress.

In today's world, Ogun is in charge of all weapons and modes of transportation; surgery; architecture; and gold, silver, and all other metals. From cab driver to construction worker, from surgeon to jeweler, from miner to pilot, all should pay homage to the orisa in charge of their jobs.

OBATALA

A o ro fo l ese Obatala l Orun.

We shall state our case before
Obatala in heaven.

Banta-banta n'nu ala!
O sun n nu ala,
O ji n nu ala,
O tinu ala dide
Ba nla! Oko Yemowo!
Orisa wu mi ni budo
Ibi re lorisha kale.

Immense in white robes!
He sleeps in white clothes,
He wakes in white clothes,
He rises in white clothes.
Worshiped Father! Yemowo's
  husband!
Orisa delights me as he is in
  place;
It is a wonderful place where
  orisa is enthroned.

—YORUBA PRAYER TO
  OBATALA

TEN

OBATALA

Obatala may well be your guardian orisa if

▲ you are more cerebral than physical
▲ you love ideas
▲ you have a strong sense of justice and honor
▲ your nerves are easily frayed
▲ you prefer small groups to large parties
▲ people seek out your opinions
▲ you prefer to be monogamous
▲ you prefer classical or "quiet" music to rock or rap
▲ you enjoy watching the news
▲ you are always analyzing other people's behavior and motives
▲ you need periods of being alone
▲ you prefer to stay home rather than travel
▲ you have difficulty with highly spiced foods
▲ you have more than your share of headaches and head colds

EBOS FOR OBATALA   Cool water, coconuts, milk, honey, shea butter, rice, mild cigars, bread, and cookies are all acceptable fare to this somewhat physically delicate orisa. Snails, particularly large African land snails, or *igbin,* are a delicacy for Obatala. Kola nuts are also acceptable. Liquor is *never* offered and is a strict taboo for Obatala. White doves are offered, but the blood is never placed on the stones of Obatala. Unlike every other orisa, Obatala is not offered palm oil.

SPECIAL EBOS FOR OBATALA'S CHILDREN   Because the children of Obatala (myself included) must take care of their heads, and because we are often prone to feeling the excesses of stress and deadlines, we tend to run "hot." What this means, in simple terms, is that we get overburdened or overloaded with work or responsibilities and begin to react badly to the mental pressure. A simple way of relieving this pressure is to purchase two coconuts. Offer one to Obatala. Punch two holes through the "eyes," allowing the liquid inside to drain into a glass or cup. Rub this liquid firmly into your scalp, with particular emphasis on the crown of your head. Ask Obatala to bring you peace and tranquillity while you are doing this. Leave the liquid on your hair for several hours or overnight. The calming effects are profound.

Obatala's day is Sunday.

OBATALA
//////////

O batala is king of the orisa. He is the essence of purity, justice, and clear thinking. In one sense he is the most rational, most linear of the orisa. He also represents the pure and calm way to transcendence.

In Ifa mythology, Obatala is probably known as much for his weaknesses as for his strengths. With all the orisa, enormous strengths are balanced by equally powerful potential weaknesses. Though Obatala's clarity is essential to his accumulation of wisdom and his dispensing of justice, the clouding or distortion of this clarity can have disastrous results. One of the classic myths in Ifa has to do with Obatala's "fall from grace."

Though only Oludumare could give life to human beings, it was one of Obatala's tasks to mold from clay the human figures. After a suitable number were molded, Oludumare would appear and breathe life into them. One day Obatala overindulged in palm wine and while intoxicated proceeded to ineptly and carelessly mold a group of these human figures. Some of the figures were missing arms, others legs, and those with all their appendages intact still showed imperfections somewhere. Because of his trust in Obatala's sense of duty, attention to detail, and personal integrity, Oludumare did not examine the figures when he paused to breathe life into them. From that moment in time, and from Obatala's transgression, come all the dwarves, hunchbacks, cripples, and other deformed persons. And, from that time on, because of the incredible remorse Obatala felt, they became his *omo* orisa, his children, and are sacred to him.

Pregnant women will be heard to say, *Korisa yana ire lo nio!* or "May Obatala create for us a good work of art."

For those who, like myself, find this orisa of white energy to be their personal guardian, it is essential that this tale be taken seriously. I recognize that we in the West grow up thinking that everything spiritual is a parable or allegory of our everyday lives, but the qualities of the orisa of Ifa are *not* allegorical. They are our specific and detailed instructions for tapping into and using our nonlinear energy. So, just as Obatala's positive attributes can geometrically increase our potential and accomplishments, so too can his weaknesses lead to our own emotional or physical failure. In relation to the palm wine tale, it is invariably true that the children of Obatala must be careful regarding overindulgence or substance abuse. Obatala himself was warned of this when he descended to Earth.

In the sacred text of Ifa, Odu Otura-tutu reads,

> Palm oil separately, white cloth separately, was divined for Obatala when he was coming from Heaven to be enthroned in the world. He was told to sacrifice: white wrapping cloth, snail, and 20,000 cowries. He was advised not to drink palm wine at all. He obeyed but sacrificed only halfway. He was told to clothe himself in white cloth. "White cloth is the dress of the orisa." He was told to wear it into the world. He was wearing white cloth but did not heed the palm oil warning. He got drunk, and palm oil splashed and stained his clothes. He then sacrificed a snail and at last vowed never to drink these wines in shame.

One of the reasons Obatala's children have so much trouble with alcohol and drugs is that they are the most linear of the nonlinear orisa. Though children of Ogun, Osun, Yemonja, Sango, and Oya have almost instantaneous call on virtually unlimited emotional energy, Obatala's energy is derived from clarity and peace. In our scientific and technological world there is little time for introspection, calmness, clarity, and peace. We are continually rushing off to something.

For the children of many of the orisa, this constant activity and pressure does not interfere with their ability to access and remain strong from their other sources of energy. For Obatalas, the persistence of such conditions over a long period of time cuts them off from the energy they need to remain productive, stable, and emotionally balanced. As the rush becomes greater and the pressures mount, the need for nonlinear sources of energy becomes more and more desperate—and less and less accessible. Under these conditions children of Obatala who are unaware of how to tap into orisa energy will instinctively look for ways to mute or dull the constant input. They may be tempted by drugs and alcohol as ways of achieving that peace, but these means will always be ultimately destructive. If you are a child of Obatala, you should take this warning quite seriously.

Similarly, though the children of Esu, Oya, Osun, and Sango can party all day and night, those who are guided by Obatala simply can't handle it. If they attempt to, it will erode their ability to accomplish the tasks for which they are uniquely qualified. Even large groups tend to "frazzle" Obatalas. Though they can certainly deal with the social milieu and even thrive in it for short periods, the children of Obatala must know when to back off and seek some time alone, some contemplative time.

Obatala controls the head. For that reason the children of Obatala must be careful about their heads in both practical and spiritual matters. When the head is "safe" it will provide the strengths of reason, planning, clarity, humility, and ethical understanding. When it is "hot" it will confuse, alarm, and disrupt one's everyday life. In order to achieve a healthy state it is again essential that those who are guided by Obatala construct a life that includes rest and quiet periods for being alone.

Obatalas are most comfortable in the woods or mountains and should plan their vacations there because their primary energy connections can best be replenished from these sources in nature. Perhaps another reason why his children enjoy the woods, hills, and mountains is that they need to avoid prolonged exposure to the sun.

In nature, Obatala is symbolized by the chameleon, gorilla, and elephant. The elephant possesses many of Obatala's characteristics. It is long lived, as should be the children of the white orisa; it has enormous power but uses it judiciously rather than capriciously, and it successfully lives a life unbothered by other animals. The gorilla is one of the most intelligent of animals, lives on the mountainside, and is basically shy. The chameleon lives on low branches in the forest and has a special affinity for Obatala. The chameleon's survival and defense is based on cunning and stealth, and its ability to change color and avoid capture is likened to Obatala's wisdom for accomplishing the same thing.

The land snail, or *igbin,* also has a special affinity for Obatala. One of the oldest life forms on the mountain, its cool secretions and blood are powerful medicines for cooling and treating one's head. As children of Obatala must guard against loss of sight, head injuries, and cerebral accidents, the medicinal value of the land snail's soothing secretions cannot be overestimated. The *igbin* has great importance throughout the mythology of Ifa.

Obatala uses no magic. He prefers to use reason and wisdom to accomplish his goals. But if one is too intransigent or refuses to "see the light," Obatala's companion Esu steps in and punishes for him.

Obatala is also the judge. He was chosen by Oludumare to make the right decisions. Some people have assumed that this aspect is simply an extension of his role as "king of the orisa." In actuality, it is his coolness of thought that caused Oludumare to appoint him administrator of justice. This ability to make cool, rational decisions is a primary attribute of Obatala. Its down side is that Obatalas tend to "administer" justice on a continual basis! Often the children of Obatala will not recognize that they are constantly passing judgment. Frankly, it just doesn't occur to them that you might not want to hear that there is a "better" route to the store or a more efficient method for accomplishing your task. Making it even more annoying is that they are almost invariably correct! What Obatalas must come to grips with and learn to recognize—if they are to use their strengths in a productive fashion—is that everyone need not always do things in the most *efficient* manner. Indeed, for the children of most other orisa, pressure to find the most efficient way of doing something would just detract from their enjoyment of it. Obatalas must learn that, for others, most efficient is not necessarily best.

Obatala's stomach is as delicate as his head. Though the warrior orisa will delight in hot peppers, cayenne, and spices of every kind, Obatala will make his life vastly more comfortable by eating blandly and sensibly. Milk, honey, rice, yam, or breads are often offered to the shrines of Obatala, along with coconuts, bananas, and fresh fruits. His children would do well to adhere to a milder and more reasoned diet as well.

All this is in no way meant to imply that Obatala or his children are in any way effete; Obatala possesses and dispenses great strength. It is simply an acknowledgment that in his specificity as an orisa—and all orisa are different—his strength is derived and nurtured through a much different process.

Obatala has both male and female aspects. In one of his female paths he is known as Ochanla, an old and wise female. In others he has a propensity toward shells or making money. In still others he is the teacher or in charge of the head. Yet whatever particular path of Obatala you are destined to follow, the general characteristics will remain the same.

Despite Obatala's need for periods of quiet, his inherent judgmental behavior, and his need to avoid alcohol and drugs, he remains an orisa with a great sense of humor. Yet his humor, like all other aspects of his existence, is unique to him. His is the humor of having seen so much, of having so much knowledge, such genuine understanding and empathy for the human condition, that laughter becomes an extension of understanding. Laughter replaces anger; tolerance replaces impetuosity.

SANGO

On'-ile ina!   The Lord of the house of fire!
A da ni ni ji   One who causes sudden dread!
Ina osan!   Noonday fire!
Ina gun ori ile fe ju!   Fire that mounts the roof and becomes glaring
    flame!
Ebiti re firi se gbi!   The murderous weight that strikes the ground
    with resounding force!

—YORUBA PRAYER TO SANGO

ELEVEN
//////////

SANGO

Sango may well be your guardian orisa if

▲ you are extremely articulate
▲ you can talk people into whatever you want
▲ you are always looking ahead at the probability of people's actions
▲ you have had experiences with the dead
▲ you often have premonitions that come true
▲ you have strong reactions to thunderstorms
▲ you love dance and music
▲ people either love or dislike you
▲ you often set the trend for your friends or family
▲ you are highly sexual
▲ you love the color red
▲ you have a quick temper
▲ you are physically attractive
▲ you enjoy physical activity
▲ you "cut corners"

EBOS TO SANGO   Six red apples, placed on a dish and set upon a shelf in your home, are a standard offering. Red palm oil, available at African food stores, is a staple that can be offered as well. Sango also enjoys spicy foods, so a plate of peppers or a portion of highly seasoned chili would make an excellent offering. Sango is the only orisa that does not take kola nuts, except for the bitter kola nut. If you are able to obtain kola nuts at a local specialty store, be certain that you specify *bitter* kola for your Sango sacrifice. Rooster and ram are blood offerings to Sango. It is often pleasant to light a candle at the same time you make your offering. This candle can be any color (other than black), but a white candle is most commonly used. Some traditions recommend a red candle for Sango, but it is not necessary. When you make your offering ask Sango for the specific help you need. If it is possible, make your offering during a thunderstorm.

Sango's day is Thursday.

SANGO

////////////

ango (pronounced Zhan-GO) is both the child of Yemonja and a former king, or Alafin, of Oyo. Because he is the child of Yemonja, no ritual act to him can be considered complete without an offering to her as well. He is best known as the orisa of thunder and lightning. But in fact the gift of lightning was not originally his; it was a skill he learned from his first wife, Oya. Indeed, Sango's path, both as man-orisa and later as orisa-man, is inextricably intertwined with Oya.

In the mythology that depicts Sango as the fourth ruler of Oyo, he was married to the beautiful and powerful Oya. Sango was always a man of quick and vociferous temper, whose verbal rage transmuted into the thunder for which he is known. It was Oya who provided him with the magic medicine for the secret of producing both thunder and lightning. It was also the mystical Oya who advised him on the plot to manipulate his two powerful generals, Gboonkaa and Timi, into mutual conflict. Oya assured him that in so doing, the generals would destroy each other, leaving Sango the unchallenged ruler of Oyo.

But the best-laid plans of even future orisa sometimes go astray, and when the predicted conflict actually took place, it was Gboonkaa who emerged victorious and with greater power than before. He used this power to topple Sango and drive him from Oyo. Oya, Sango's loyal wife, followed him into exile. She had urged him to return to the grasslands near the Niger River, which was later to bear her name and her mystical power, but Sango was so remorseful over the mistakes he had made, felt such contrition at his previous dictatorial behavior, that he

Sango priestess in front of a family altar filled primarily with Ibeji (twin) figures in honor of generation upon generation of twins in her family, 1950.

hanged himself from an aayon tree. When those who had been his followers heard of his fate and rushed to see his body, nobody was found hanging there. Sango, in his act of remorse and contrition, had exceeded the human condition and transcended to become Orisa Sango!

Today, one of the most popular prayers for this powerful orisa remains:

Oba ko so.

The king did not hang.

Sango's energy is intense and powerful. Perhaps more than with any other orisa, it applies to a wide spectrum of capabilities. Sango is the general, the born leader. His fierceness is widely acknowledged, and most fear his wrath. He is known for his double-headed ax, which he wields in battle. But though best known as a warrior, Sango is, in reality, the quintessential strategist. His strategy sometimes goes awry, as in his earthly attempt to destroy his two powerful generals by pitting them against each other, but over the many years his knack for strategy has become highly refined and almost unstoppable. Sango and his children are simply born manipulators. And though they will go to battle ferociously, they will do it only as a last resort. Sangos love nothing better than to plan ahead—to set the stage and pull the strings necessary to produce the results they desire. Sangos who are in touch with their energy will get people to do exactly what they want but leave them with the impression that they made their own decisions.

Manipulation can surely be used for good or evil, and, like all energy, Sango's has a positive and negative side. Sangos using their energy in a nonproductive manner can wreak havoc. Though history's greatest chess champions were undoubtedly omo Sango, so too were its greatest con artists! Part of this is explained by Sango's great gift of gab. Children of Sango can be hypnotic speakers. The great political orators, from Mark Anthony to William Jennings Bryan, were almost certainly omo Sango.

Because of Sango's ability to solve problems, he and his children seem to be drawn to them. Omo Sango's lives seem to be more filled with difficulties than most, but their problem-solving capacities quickly sweep their troubles away. And they are in constant demand to solve other people's problems as well. In fact, if omo Sango are not careful, too much of their time and energy will be consumed with other people's troubles, leaving them insufficient time to travel their own paths.

Sango's powers of empathy and intuition cannot be overstated. Early *oriki* (little prayers and stories) suggest that at one time it was Sango who possessed the divination board and the secret of casting the future. In these stories it is said that because of his inborn ability to sense future events Sango felt no need to use the physical equipment and techniques and so traded them to Orunmila in exchange for the gift of dancing.

Feats of the supernatural are commonplace to Sango and his children. They also seem to have a natural affinity for and regular contact with the dead. Many of Sango's supernatural abilities come forth during his display of *p'idon,* or magic, at his annual festival. The head Sango priest, or *eleeegun,* assisted by other initiates, enters a trance and proceeds to perform a series of acts that have been done precisely in this way since the beginning of time. These include placing fire on their heads, holding it in their mouths, and then spitting it forth in a reflection of the lightning that is his counterpart in nature. Often the priest's abdomen is pierced with a slender knife, his tongue pierced with an iron nail, and perhaps most impressive, his eyeball removed, cut off, and then replaced in its socket. It is critical to understand that these feats are not sleight-of-hand or trickery; they are psychokinetically controlled actions while in trance by the highest level of Sango priest. They are dynamic substantiations of the powerful and violent energy that is Sango.

Sango's children communicate with their guardian by shaking a small gourd, or *sere*. This communication became possible when Sere, a gourd native to western Nigeria, found that she had no one to serve. Her sister gourd, Igba, was serving Oya, and her other sister, Akingbe, was serving Odo. Sere sought the services of a babalawo to help her. Her odu was Ose Meji. The babalawo instructed Sere on a certain herbal preparation that contained, among other ingredients, beans and seeds of various plants. She was told to prepare the ebo and to eat it. Immediately after eating it she was to go to the nearest Sango shrine and pray to the orisa. Sere followed the instructions and, upon eating the sacred medicine, went immediately to the nearest Sango shrine, where she threw herself on the ground shouting the praises of Sango. As she threw herself before the shrine, the nuts and seeds she had consumed made a strange rattling sound in her stomach. Sango heard this strange noise and was delighted with it. Sango called out,

> There is no other in my kingdom like you.
>
> I will dance through my realm.
>
> You, Sere, will always proceed me,
>
> you will call them with your unique sound,
>
> you will say, Sakasiki, Sikasaka, Sikasiki, Sakasaka!

Afterward, wherever Sango went in his kingdom, he was preceded by Sere. When his followers heard her strange sound they would know Sango was about to appear. Sere, in her gratitude to odu Ose Meji that he had allowed her, too, to find service, included Ose's name in her call. Her sound became Osesakasiki, Osesikisaka, Ose, Ose, Ose.

Today, when Sango's followers wish to call upon their orisa, they pick up Sere and shake her until the sound of Osesakasiki, Osesikisaka, transcends the moment and calls forth the potent energy of Sango.

The ram is symbolic of Sango, and its horns are used for his altar. The ram is also the primary blood sacrifice for appeasing or invoking intervention by this powerful orisa. Yet the association of Sango with the ram offers great insight into genuine Sango energy. The ram is quick and determined, yet it does not have the teeth or claws of a carnivore, which are designed to maim and kill. It may give a nasty butt to those who offend it, but it does not seek to kill or destroy.

The snake is regarded as Sango's messenger. Its lightning-shaped body corresponds with Sango's most visible physical manifestation. The crocodile is also closely associated with Sango because the loud cracking of its reptilian eggs is akin to the thunder that accompanies Sango's fiery bolts. The ax, both single- and double-headed, is the constant companion of this warrior orisa. The single-headed ax, known as *ake* Sango, is much rarer than the double-headed ax, or *oshe* Sango, that he is normally seen carrying. As important as his axes are the thunderstones or celts that are invariably carried in small leather waist bags by Sango priests. Children of Sango are well advised to carry this teardrop-shaped stone, which is said to be the residue from the thunderbolt that Sango casts from above. Many tales abound as to how Sango destroys his enemies by hurling his bolts, and it is believed that each one that is dug up and found carries with it not only the mystical power of Sango but the accumulated *asé* or energy of the vanquished enemy.

Among Ifa devotees, any house or structure that is struck with lightning must be examined and cleansed by Sango priests before it can be safely inhabited again. This process cannot be completed until the attending priest and his followers discover and remove the thunderstone that remains from the carnage.

But Sango is not only a potent force of destruction. He is a force for procreation as well. He is to male fertility what Osun is to female conception. Sango is highly sexual and tends to have numerous satisfying relationships. His children, if in touch with their energy, will be highly sexual as well. Celibacy or long periods of abstinence from sexual activity would drain the Sango energy. Sango is also the male deity for twins. When Sango took his wife, Osun, to his brass palace, she bore him twins. From that time on, Sango became the male orisa of multiple births. If you are a twin, your guardian orisa will be either Sango or Osun.

As children are the ultimate blessing of Ifa, the birth of twins is obviously a double blessing. For those who doubt the importance of orisa energy in the conception of children in general, and the Sango and Osun energy in the birth of twins in particular, ponder for a moment the fact that the Yoruba bear twins thirty times as often as the rest of the world!

Sango energy carries with it the absence of ambivalence. What Sango and his children will never encounter is a person or a group who feels neutrally toward them. Instead, the lives of omo Sango will be filled with people who look up to and follow their every lead and with people who seem to have an inborn dislike for them. This dislike is more than just casual; it more likely stems from some primeval events in which Sango energy negatively affected several other energy sources. For example, Sango has a long history of conflicts with Ogun, the taciturn warrior orisa of all metals. Not the least of these was Ogun's loss of Oya, his wife, to the more handsome and social Sango. Though relationships between children of the two orisa are possible, they will be based more on mutual fear than on respect.

Although some orisa energies blend better than others, and some are more (or less) likely to get along, it is important to understand that orisa energy is not only attracted to like energy but is often best balanced by an opposite energy. That is well demonstrated in the mythic tale of Obatala and Sango.

Obatala was planning a trip from his kingdom of Ife to visit Sango in the neighboring kingdom of Oyo. He consulted with the Ifa oracle before undertaking the journey. Ifa informed Obatala that he could meet death on the proposed journey. If he wished to avoid death he must be prepared to suffer a number of insults and indignities along the way, and he should do so without complaint. So warned, Obatala began his journey. Time after time he was confronted by the mischievous Esu in a variety of disguises. Each time Esu attempted to provoke Obatala into a conflict through insults and humiliations. Each time Obatala heeded the advice of Orunmila and stoically continued on his journey.

Finally, after an almost unbearable series of confrontations, he arrived in the kingdom of Oyo. The first thing he saw was Sango's horse running wild after obviously escaping from confinement. He managed to catch the runaway horse and was holding its reins when Sango's soldiers arrived. They immediately took Obatala as the thief who had stolen the horse and unceremoniously threw him into prison. Soon afterward a series of calamities struck Sango's kingdom of Oyo: crops failed, people fought, children died, women could not conceive. Sango consulted with Orunmila in order to save his kingdom. Ifa informed him that the cause of Oyo's trouble was an innocent old man who was being held in jail. Sango himself hurried to the prison, where he recognized his old friend Obatala and begged his forgiveness. The two reunited as old and close friends, and Oyo once again prospered. Obatala had suffered silently as instructed by Ifa and avoided death.

How can Obatala and Sango be such close friends with such opposite energies? The coolness, wisdom, and calm of Obatala serve to balance rather than challenge the spontaneity, anger, and ceaseless energy of Sango.

The color red is favored by Sango and his priests. Their hair is worn in a plaited, almost feminine, fashion, which seems in direct contradiction to the ultramasculinity of the Sango energy. Indeed, this male energy is so forceful that all of his children, be they male or female, are known as *sons* of Sango!

Children of Sango often use the time during a severe thunderstorm to communicate with their primary orisa force, and, in a melding of technology with transcendence, urban omo Sango would do well to place a negative ion machine in their homes or places of business. These negative ions—now replicable through electronics—are the residue that remains after the air is charged by Sango lightning. The beneficial effects of these negatively charged particles have even been substantiated by modern science! They are the reason we love to breathe the fresh, crisp air after a storm. These ions are simply a quantifiable aspect of the power and positive force of Sango.

YEMONJA/OLUKUN

Ategbe, Ategbe awo Olukun li o difa f'Olukun. Aguta atu egbaa mesan owo li ebo, won ni a di alaje, a di olmo. O Gbo o ru. O di Alaje, o di Olomo ati beebee.

Ategbe, Ategbe, Olukun's babalawo divined for Olukun. Olukun was told to sacrifice a sheep and ten thousand cowries to become rich and have many children. Olukun did these things and flourished as predicted.

—IRETE OGBE

112

TWELVE

YEMONJA/OLUKUN

You may well be a child of Yemonja/Olukun if

- ▲ you love children
- ▲ you have a genuine caring feeling for other people
- ▲ you are slow to anger
- ▲ you prefer to stay home with your family rather than go out and party
- ▲ you are attracted to lakes, streams, or the ocean
- ▲ you are basically calm
- ▲ you have an exceptional, but seldom expressed, temper
- ▲ you tend to be slightly heavy
- ▲ you easily see another person's point of view
- ▲ you forgive easily and often
- ▲ you are exceptionally protective about your children
- ▲ money is easy for you to make but not your foremost consideration
- ▲ emotional sustenance is more important than material objects
- ▲ people are drawn to you for comfort and understanding
- ▲ you are sensual in a quiet rather than overt fashion

EBOS FOR YEMONJA/OLUKUN   Fruits, particularly red or purple grapes, melons, squash, beer, gin, rum, candy, and cakes are all staple offerings. Watermelon is a favorite of this deep-water orisa. Palm oil, kola nuts, coral, and flowers can all be used as offerings. Sheep, guinea fowl, hens, pigeons, raw or cooked fish, and palm wine are also acceptable.

Yemonja/Olukun's day is Monday.

YEMONJA / OLUKUN
//////////

In the beginning of time, when Oludumare created Earth, Yemonja/Olukun existed as the primal oceans on the earth's uninhabited surface. The Sun descended upon and forcibly took Yemonja/Olukun. From this act, fifteen orisa were born, and Yemonja became the Mother of Earth. It is also told that from this action powerful streams of sweet water sprang from her breasts, creating the freshwater lakes and streams of the earth. All life is nurtured and sustained by her. In her female mothering aspect she is identified as Yemonja. Her male aspect is the powerful and often feared Olukun. This makes neither her nor him, nor their followers, schizophrenic. It merely recognizes, in all orisa as in all life, the male-female dichotomy, the light and the darkness, the nurturer and the warrior. It is not only the reality of Yemonja/Olukun, it is yours and mine as well.

Yemonja/Olukun is often referred to in the syncretized traditions as the personification of motherhood. This description is wholly inadequate. You must always remember that the orisa are forces of energy, sources that exist not only in nature but in your own body as well. Each and every one of us is part animal, part mineral, part vegetable. We are as much the water, rock, iron, tree, or lion as we are human beings. It is in this sense that Yemonja/Olukun—like all the orisa—lives in us.

To understand and connect with your Yemonja/Olukun energy you must tap the feeling of total peace and safety that the child feels sucking at its mother's breast. Remember that feeling of overwhelming

Epa mask with figure of a pregnant Yemonja with baby on her back, from the main shrine of the palace in Oshogbo, Nigeria, 1950.

peace and comfort, that pervasive security that enveloped and protected you as an infant from the harsh realities of later life. Allow yourself to be swept up in the complete and total love of the mother for her child. Feel both the pleasure and pride the mother feels as well as her vigilant sense of protectiveness toward her young. Remember the first nightmare that sent you fleeing into your mother's arms, and recall the relief, peace, and safety you felt upon being enveloped by her. If you can remember and touch these emotions, you will be close to connecting with the Yemonja part of your character.

In the New World syncretization of Ifa into Santeria, Candomble, and related traditions, Yemonja/Olukun has been split into two entities: Yemonja *and* Olukun. There is great danger in separating the characteristics of the single Yemonja/Olukun; quite simply, each half is incomplete. Those who feel that Yemonja alone is their guardian orisa tend to be too passive, too nurturing, too caring—often at the expense of their own well-being. If you sense that you are being taken advantage of, and you have connected only with the Yemonja aspect of Yemonja/Olukun, you might not have the strength, anger, or power to set things right. It is only when you incorporate Olukun energy that you are able to feel the full range of your powers. The reverse would be equally true. Joan of Arc was probably dominated by Olukun.

In her female aspect Yemonja/Olukun is given credit for the birth of Sango, orisa of thunder and lightning; Ogun, owner of all metals and instruments made from metal; Oya, the marketplace and tornado; and Osun, sweet water, love, and wealth. Motherhood is, therefore, an exceptionally important facet of the major orisa.

Though Yemonja/Olukun is indeed the quintessential mother, she is not specifically in charge of the act of conception. That particular power is left to her daughter Osun. Once the conception has taken place and the pregnancy has been completed, Osun's work is done, and Yemonja/Olukun often takes over. Indeed, a long-standing Yoruba tale explains how Osun loves to conceive and have children but quickly tires of the responsibility of raising them. She therefore hands her children over to Yemonja/Olukun to be raised so she can go on about her own pleasures. In the orisa view of the universe this is neither "bad" nor "good," neither irresponsible nor responsible. It is simply the way things are, and it acknowledges that Osun's energy would ultimately be diminished by the twenty-four-hour-a-day nurturing of children. Yemonja/Olukun, however, would be sustained and enriched by the very same acts.

In Africa, Yemonja is represented by the Ogun River rather than by the ocean as she is in the New World. Olukun has come to reflect the bottom or mysterious part of the ocean. To understand as much of the Olukun energy as possible, visualize the utter stillness and depth of the ocean bottom. Here, separated from the rest of the world's sound and light, is the domicile of Olukun. It is here that secrets are preserved and kept, that the unknown is knowable, and that riches and treasures of the world abound. If you can envision the enormous pressure, the utter silence, the total darkness of this realm miles and miles beneath the ocean's surface, you can glimpse—however briefly—the ice-cold power and strength of the Olukun energy. It is only sensible that Yemonja, the quintessential mother, the absolute care giver and nurturer, the selfless protector, would herself be balanced and protected by an implacable and mysterious balancing force. It is when the components are dealt with separately that one faces genuine danger.

In the New World, babalawos who treat the Olukun energy as a separate orisa have begun to refuse to use the traditional ocean ceremony to initiate devotees into the mysteries of Olukun. The traditional ceremony takes place in a small boat, from which close contact with the orisa can be made. But in a series of apparently unexplainable accidents, many New World babalawos met their deaths by drowning while conducting these ceremonies. The disasters became so common that more and more of them refused to venture forth into the sea with their new initiates and now perform the initiations only on land. The African babalawo would sadly shake his head at their mistakes. He would see that by choosing to deal only with the cold, implacable Olukun energy, without the balancing force of the nurturing Yemonja energy, the unknowing babalawo were stepping into an energy vortex for which there was no controlling or mediating force. By invoking only the Olukun aspect of Yemonja/Olukun energy, the New World babalawos were unleashing uncontrollable and devastating powers that often quite literally swept them away.

Yemonja/Olukun, like her daughters Osun and Oya, carries the secret and promise of riches. The treasures that exist beneath the waters were literally the currency of ancient times. The cowrie shell and the other shells used as currency came from the rivers and oceans. Tale after tale informs the initiate of the potential wealth and riches that can be obtained by "proper" dealings with the water orisa. A famous tale involves Orunmila, who, during a time when the water orisa were said to be angry with men, was informed in a dream to go to the ocean's shore and offer sacrifice. Others had been afraid to approach the awesome, angry ocean energy, but Orunmila did as instructed. After he offered the sacrifice, a huge wind began to whip the ocean into mountainous waves. Suddenly one wave, so huge that it blotted out the sky and sun, rose directly in front of Orunmila. He was afraid that he would be swept away to his death by it. Instead of sweeping him away, however, the wave hovered directly over his head and then seemed to settle gently to the shore at his feet. As the water receded back into the ocean, Orunmila looked down to see mounds of pearls and precious stones left by the water. Once again, the orisa had been appeased and humankind had been rewarded.

Both aspects of Yemonja/Olukun can be seen through this tale. The awesome power of the tidal wave, hurricane, or typhoon, all of which can sweep away human lives and works, is balanced by the caring and richness that the waters of the earth provide. Certainly without them we could not exist. So the lashing fury of the ocean storm is balanced by the gently undulating waves that rock us much as a mother rocks her baby.

Witchcraft is also associated with this water orisa, and though Yemonja/Olukun has the capacity for it, it is her daughters Osun and Oya who are the practical and feared practitioners of the art. Perhaps Yemonja/Olukun's own awesome power makes the use of witchcraft unnecessary. This power was once put to the test by Obatala when the Olukun aspect challenged Obatala for supremacy. Olukun issued a challenge to see which orisa could be more spectacularly adorned; the winner would rise above the other in the orisa hierarchy. Obatala, using his wisdom, sent the chameleon to represent him in the contest. When Olukun arose from the ocean, adorned with the finest jewels, the most incredibly beautiful garments made from the plants and seaweeds, the most unbelievable pearled shawl, he was shocked to look and see the chameleon dressed just as well. Diving back to the depths, Olukun constructed an even more glorious costume and swept upward to the surface. Once again, as he glanced across the waters, he saw the chameleon dressed as well as he. Time after time this continued, until finally Olukun was forced to concede that he could not outdo Obatala. And, this being the case, Obatala maintained higher rank than Olukun.

This myth carries with it the secret to dealing with the awesome energy of Yemonja/Olukun. You must approach it with love, respect, and intelligence if you are not to be swept away in the whirlpool of pure energy.

The priests or priestesses and children, or omo, of Yemonja/Olukun are among the kindest and most easygoing of all the orisa energy. Their nurturing, female qualities can indeed be pictured as the surface waters of the ocean and rivers. The powerful Olukun energy lies in the bottom depths and will rise to the surface only after much disturbance or interference. It will take a great deal to anger or infuriate a child of Yemonja/Olukun. They will, by nature, be forgiving and understanding.

In relationships, the children of this orisa can usually balance and do quite well with the more turbulent energy of Oya, Osun, Ogun, and Sango. Female *olorisa* (children) will be family oriented and enjoy the tasks of raising children and creating a stable home environment. Male *olorisa* will be excellent fathers, good and concerned providers, and caring husbands. Both will be less likely to be enticed by other energy sources than the children of other orisa. When matched together they may be considered "dull" by some standards, but according to the ideals and energy that motivate them they will be happy and fulfilled.

But this very tranquillity and calm, when pushed to its limits, will not only disappear, it will explode into a wrath seldom equalled by the more obviously volatile orisa. You can push quite far before an omo Yemonja/Olukun's anger is unleashed. Should you threaten their children or spouse or the stability of their homes, however, that destructive energy will rise quickly to the surface and sweep the threat away. It is not a mistake to equate the Yemonja/Olukun anger with the force of the hurricane, tidal wave, or typhoon. Each sweeps away everything that stands in its path. Once the destructiveness has passed, the undulating waves belie the act of hours before, but the devastation is no less real. Though Yemonja/Olukun will readily forgive after they have expressed their anger, they will often leave nothing *to* forgive.

In Africa, the children of Yemonja/Olukun wear necklaces of crystal-clear beads and often carry fans sacred to their cult. Seven is the number most often associated with Yemonja/Olukun. Her vessels contain sacred rocks from her depths, which have been ritually consecrated to her and are usually filled with water.

In Brazil, Yemonja/Olukun is virtually the national deity. Each year, on January 1, tens of thousands of Brazilians go to the shore of the ocean and place beautiful cakes, fruits, and candies on small hand-made boats, which are floated out as an offering to their patron orisa. At midnight these same *olorisa* will, with their backs turned toward the ocean, jump over seven incoming waves as a ritual for health and prosperity for the coming year.

In Yemonja/Olukun, Yemonja represents the "feminine" component, Olukun the "masculine." Not a contradiction, this is an affirmation of the Yoruba view of the universe, where all things contain both male and female energy. When the babalawo divines with either the *ikin* or the *opele,* he is always looking at two distinct components. The right side of the odu represents the male energy; the left represents the female. It is the relationship between the two that goes a long way toward determining exactly what is happening in a client's life. As we have seen above, separating them can have disastrous results and provides a graphic example of what happens when we try to separate the male and female forces within us all.

OYA

Eesin gbona l'ewe tutu l'egbo li o difa fun Marunlelogojo igi oko, Ope ati Ayinre li o ru: Oromodie ninu-won. Itorinaa bi iji ba nja, Ogo mariwo a ni: Oun sebo.

Eesin gbona l'ewe tutu l'egbo divined for 165 trees. Only palm tree and Ayinre sacrificed a chicken among the lot. Therefore, in time of gale or tornado that threatened other trees, young palm leaves would declare: We had sacrificed and so escaped danger.

—OYEKESE

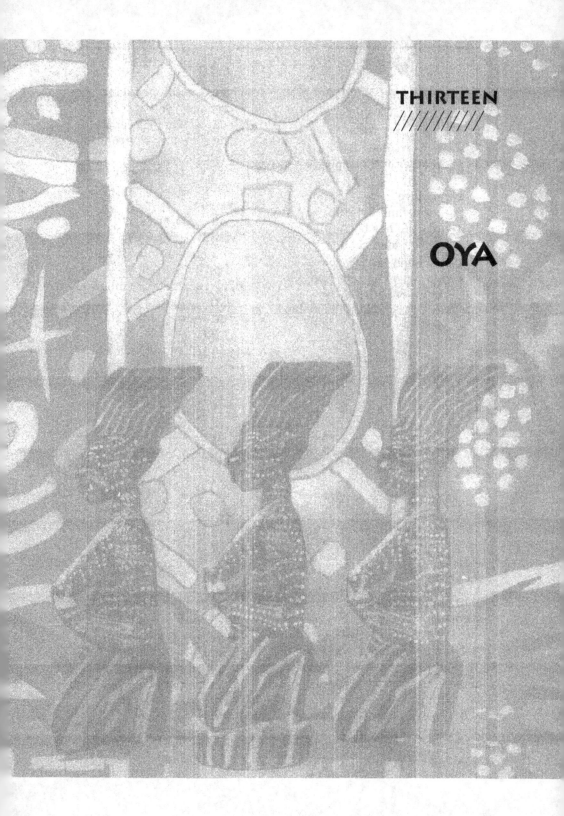

THIRTEEN
//////////

OYA

You may well be a child of Oya if

- ▲ you have sudden bursts of anger
- ▲ you have been left by a member of the opposite sex
- ▲ you love (or fear) thunderstorms and lightning
- ▲ your life has been filled with sudden change
- ▲ you enjoy darker colors
- ▲ you have had some experience or sense of the dead
- ▲ you are not bothered by funerals or cemeteries
- ▲ you are a natural gardener
- ▲ you are not afraid of physical combat
- ▲ as a woman, you enjoy the company of strong males
- ▲ as a male, you enjoy the company of strong women
- ▲ you cannot tolerate deceit or lying
- ▲ you have a natural antipathy toward the "flirty," flashy members of the opposite sex
- ▲ you were a "difficult" child
- ▲ you resent discipline or confinement

EBOS FOR OYA Eggplants are a favorite of Oya. The dark skin matches this purple orisa. Depending upon the circumstances, as many as nine may be offered at one time. Oya also loves rum, gin, beer, wine, and dark fruit such as plums and red or purple grapes. Palm oil, kola nuts, and coconuts are also suitable offerings. Hen and female goat may be offered depending upon which aspect of this female warrior orisa you are calling upon. Nine colored ribbons or the old-fashioned children's pinwheel toys, which harness and react to the wind, are also excellent for Oya.

Oya's day is Wednesday.

OYA

//////////

Oya (pronounced Oi-YA!)—first wife of Ogun, then swept away by Sango. Oya—the Niger River. Oya—the tornado and whirlwind. Oya—the marketplace. Oya—gatekeeper to the cemetery. Oya—beautiful, bearded warrior. Oya—female anger. Oya—the essence of change. Oya—difficult to know. Oya—essential to know.

Of all the orisa, Oya is probably the most difficult to fathom. In one sense, this is because a mysterious quality is essential to her energy. In another, it is because when Oya energy impacts our daily lives, it does so with such abruptness and ferocity that we would prefer to avoid the convergence rather than encourage it. Yet, for those who are children of Oya, or for those adept at tapping into her energy, the possibilities are endless.

To help understand the mysterious quality of Oya, it is important to recall her relationship with Sango. As his wife, she was truly the power behind the throne, and her "suggestions" often propelled Sango in the directions Oya felt appropriate. Perhaps some of the animosity that Sango engendered among his followers resulted from this outside influence. Ultimately, at the urging of Oya, Sango pitted his two rival generals against each other in the hope that they would destroy each other. When one survived, he drove Sango and Oya from their kingdom into exile. It was during this exodus that Sango, filled with contrition, hanged himself from a tree limb, transcended the human condition, and ascended to orisa. It was then that Oya attempted to drown herself in the Niger River out of her own sorrow and pain. She too transcended the human condition and rose to orisa.

Shrine figure of Oya from palace in Oshogbo, Nigeria, 1950.

Her desire to guide or manipulate Sango from behind the scenes is a microcosm of the mystery in the energy of this powerful orisa. Her relationship with Sango was formative in a number of ways. The New World tale of Oya "stealing" the secret of lightning and thunder from Sango when he was carousing with Osun belittles the power of this female warrior. Instead, just as Oya often led Sango in the directions she chose, so too she always possessed the power that enabled Sango to direct his bolts of destructive energy at their targets. In this way the two powerful orisa worked together—Oya setting the course and Sango delivering the blows. Thousands of years after Sango and Oya walked the earth, modern science, in an attempt to understand and protect our environment, has discovered that a microsecond before lightning occurs, a minute electrical particle is emitted that descends to Earth. The lightning that strikes a nanosecond later follows the exact path of this energy particle! In its attempt to avoid the destructiveness of thunder and lightning, the energy of these two orisa, science has actually confirmed their existence and specific roles. That minute electrical energy that precedes the lightning is Oya, once more determining the path that Sango shall follow.

More than anything, Oya represents the energy of sudden change. Her role as orisa of the marketplace is a practical example of this force. The marketplace represents commerce and trade, profits and losses. How quickly money can change hands, how suddenly good luck can produce fortunes and bad luck can dissipate them! The poor become rich, and the rich become poor. In this constant ebb and flow, this shifting current of fortune, Oya is the predominant and guiding force. Offerings to Oya are most often made at a shrine in the marketplace, and no Ifa devotee would ever think of starting a new business or beginning his or her business week without propitiating this orisa of change.

Oya, in her role as the tornado, exemplifies still another aspect of her energy of sudden change. The tornado's selective destructiveness is part of its fascination. Riding low in the storm-laden sky, she will suddenly dip and leave absolute waste where something apparently solid and substantial stood just moments before. Within inches of destroying the next home or building in her path, she will suddenly zoom upward, leaving the potential victim totally untouched. Though her destruction may seem random, it is not. Oya's wrath is always precisely exercised, and what appears random is not. Her destructiveness, as stated above, is selective. The tornado, like the marketplace, produces sudden change, sudden shifting of fortunes. It is this ability to almost instantly reverse fortunes that brings most Ifa devotees to ask that Oya spare rather than reward them.

No change is more profound than death. Though Icu, the orisa of death, remains firmly in charge of taking people when their time has come, it is Oya who is gatekeeper to the cemetery. It is totally consistent that this orisa of sudden change should be in charge of opening the gate between the marketplace and our home—between Earth and Heaven. Oya is completely comfortable with the dead. In her pervasive use of witchcraft (at which she is expert), her relationship with the dead plays an important role. One of the classic Oya/Sango tales illustrates this point:

Oya, who had left her original husband, Ogun, for the affections of Sango, discovered that Sango had become enamored with orisa Osun. This captivating goddess of love and sensuality was using her magical charms to lure Sango away from Oya. Oya was furious. She had confronted Sango with her knowledge, but he had denied everything. Finally, she took matters into her own hands. Using her powers with the dead, and understanding Sango's revulsion for them, Oya summoned forth a cadre of the dead to surround the ile (house) of Sango and keep him prisoner. Now it was Sango's turn to be angry.

"Oya," he screamed, "you cannot hold me prisoner in my own home. I have tasks in my kingdom; my subjects need me; you must call off your minions."

"The only task you are looking to perform," replied Oya, "is one with that hussy Osun! No, my husband, you will remain in your home until her charms have worn off."

And with that, Oya strode haughtily away.

Osun, hearing of her lover's confinement, waited until Oya left for the marketplace and slipped by the dead guards into Sango's ile. Once there, she dressed Sango in women's attire and went out to distract the guards. So great are Osun's charms that even the dead are not immune to them, and while they were flirting with the orisa of sensuality, Sango slipped away.

When Oya returned from the marketplace and discovered that her husband had escaped with Osun, she was beside herself. Sango, in his haste, had made a tragic error; he had left behind his instruments of fire and thunder. In her anger Oya entered Sango's private sanctuary and discovered his magical gourd and mortar and pestle. Dipping her finger into the gourd she felt a pastelike substance. She brought the finger to her mouth and felt a searing heat. The shout that she emitted was almost as shocking as the fire that accompanied it. The jagged flame of lightning that came from her mouth was Sango's secret of fire. The mortar and pestle yielded the secret of thunder, and now this already powerful female warrior became even more powerful.

Eventually, Sango and Oya reached a kind of mutual understanding. The great love they had once held for each other could no longer exist, but the two would work together in the casting of thunderbolts and the destruction of enemies. The loss of love had been compensated for, in part, by the acquisition of greater knowledge and power.

From this tale comes another insight into orisa Oya. Her resentment of men and her eternal dislike for Osun now make sense!

It is said of Oya:

A-su-jo ma ro.

She causes a heavy dark cloud but brings no rain.

It is important to understand the strength and determination of the female orisa of Ifa. Though a basically chauvinistic attitude has become part of nearly all religions and cultures, the male and female orisa of Ifa were separate but equal. It was, therefore, not a cowering, docile Oya who crept into Sango's sanctuary to seize the secret of thunder and lightning; it was a fiercely proud, angry, and offended woman. It is this pride and anger that still prevail in the energy of Oya and her children.

Oya carries a sword in each hand. They speak of her love of truth and honesty. It is these characteristics that she still shares with her first husband, Ogun, from whom she took instruments of war when she left him for Sango. Indeed, these instruments often adorn the omo Oya in the form of necklaces or bracelets.

Oya's children are identified by strings of dark red beads, and the number nine is most often associated with this proud orisa. Oya is propitiated with female goats, and her devotees wear attire similar to that of Sango priests. Their ritual dress consists of many layers of kilts or often one stiff, leather, apronlike covering. Vests beaded with cowries speak of her control of the fortunes of men and often extend from chest to ankle. She is the mother of Egungun, or ancestor mask, and priests and priestesses of Oya often wear elaborate masks to conceal their identities.

Oya shares thunderstones or celts with Sango, but hers are more rounded, not pointed or sharp as are Sango's. Often the omo Oya will wear these rounded thunderstones on chains around their necks. Some will also be placed at the sacred shrine of Oya. The *igba* gourd is shaken to communicate with Oya, and its sound replicates the storm and wind.

Another aspect of Oya that requires understanding is her role as a warrior. Though all the female orisa of Ifa have powerful energy sources, Oya, exclusive among her sisters, will enter battle side by side with the male orisa. In this aspect Oya is viewed as the bearded female warrior whose wrath and power sweep all injustice, deceit, and dishonesty from her path. That is why Oya is often called "the woman who grows a beard on account of war."

Her unique ability to function equally with males in battle derives from her possession of the tools of war, which she took from Ogun, and her knowledge of the secret of thunder and lightning, which she learned from Sango. When these tools are combined with her sense of outrage and justice, warrior Oya is a feared and formidable opponent.

What does all this mean to the children of Oya? First and foremost, omo Oya are volatile in nature. The energy of this orisa simply cannot be suppressed for any significant length of time. When male or female Oyas are angered, they will express it in dramatic and often tornadic style.

Thus they are often called

Efufulele ti da gi l oke-l-oke.

The rushing wind that tears down trees from the top.

As children they will be difficult to control, insisting upon their own tastes and setting their own agendas. Their tantrums will spring full-blown from seemingly innocuous situations, and calming them will be harder than expected. In adults, however, this same energy can be captivating and charming. Usually dark-complexioned, they possess a certain sensuality that often belies their outward appearance. This sensuality tends to be somewhat restrained or self-composed, however. It is almost as if the hurt felt by Oya over Sango's indiscretions with Osun has permanently colored her view of relationships. For this reason it will take extraordinarily persevering men or women to wear down the inherent skepticism of the Oya they love. In matters of loyalty and dependability, no orisa can match Oya. Children of Oya, once committed, will remain loyal unless deceived or lied to.

Oya, because of her relationship with the dead, is one of the only orisa that likes and adorns herself with dark colors. Her children, as well, are not adversely affected by wearing them. Purples, reds, maroons, even black are totally acceptable for the omo Oya; black would be taboo for omo Obatalas and improper for other orisa. Generally, her children will have experienced contact with the dead. The children of Oya have such a strong connection with the dead that it would be rare to find one that has not had memorable dreams of the departed or at least a sense that spirits are around.

Her children will also be naturally adept at witchcraft or magic. It is told how Osonyin, the orisa of herbs and magic, refused to share his knowledge with the other orisa. Once again it was the courage of Oya that restored balance. Finding that Osonyin had hidden a huge magical gourd filled with his herbal secrets of magic at the top of a huge tree, she caused ferocious winds to blow, which in turn caused the gourd to fall and spill some of its contents on the forest floor. Even though Osonyin managed to gather up the majority of his treasures, each orisa managed to obtain a few of the herbal secrets for him- or herself. Though they must always pay homage to Osonyin, the orisa know and appreciate that Oya made some of the secrets available to them. Because of this, Oya has access to all their knowledge, and her use of herbal magic is surpassed only by that of Osonyin himself. Her children will often have a natural affinity toward herbs or plants, and those with a natural "green thumb" may well be omo Oya.

Oya's children should also have little difficulty making money. As owner of the marketplace she allows her children to tap into the positive energy that makes commercial activities highly successful. Omo Oya would do extremely well in any retail operation, in stock or commodity speculation, or in marketing. Their energy would be diminished by sitting behind a computer, teaching, or providing health care or medical care. Oya energy requires movement and change, and the ability to thrive under those circumstances is responsible for Oya's success.

As owner of the wind, Oya is also owner of the air we breathe. Those with respiratory problems would do well to see what offering might be acceptable to Oya to relieve them of their difficulties.

Oya is an orisa of power and action. Even the pronunciation of her name requires a strong accent on the last syllable. It is not *Oya,* it is *OYA!*

The sound should carry a strong exhalation of air and duplicate, as closely as possible, the force and strength of the strong wind she represents.

The greatest difficulty her children face will have to do with tempering their violent reactions and mood swings. Today's omo Oya! must learn to express anger or displeasure, but not to lay waste everything in its path. Once control of this aspect of our nature has been accomplished, the laserlike energy of this warrior orisa can bring us riches and accomplishments beyond our dreams.

OSUN

Osekeseke li o difa f'aje,
won ni tire sa ni gbogbo aye yoo
   mafi se oni ise.
A niki o ba le re bee,
ohungbogbo ti enu i je ne ebo.
Aje gbo o ru.
Gbogbo aye si nyo le Aje sekeseke.

Her cooling waters heal
the mother of mothers
she removes infertility.
That which was barren will
swell from her waters.
That which was poor can become
   wealthy.
Merriment divined for wealth,
   who was told that
the whole world would always be
   in search of her.
She was asked to sacrifice
   anything edible, which she did.
As a result, the whole world is
   happy to be in search of her.

—OSE MEJI

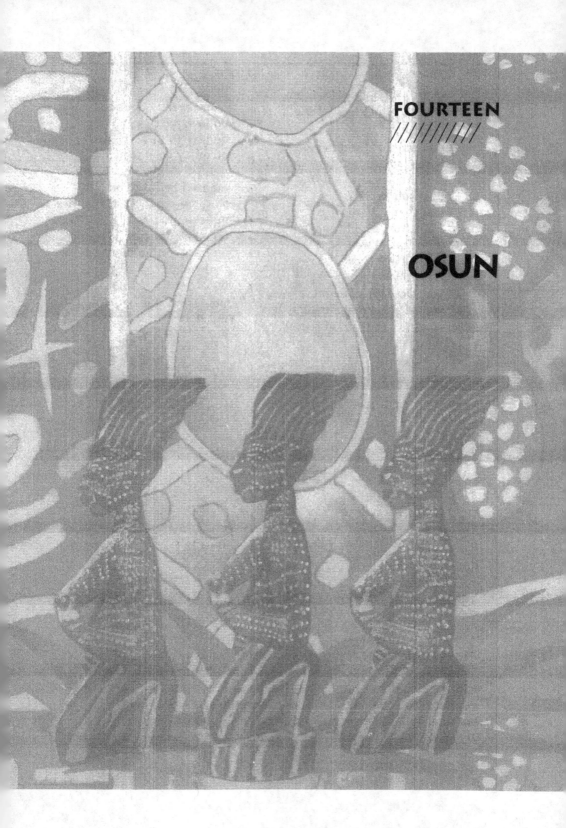

FOURTEEN

OSUN

Osun may be your guardian orisa if

- ▲ you cannot stand to be bored
- ▲ you are acutely aware of how you look
- ▲ you spend more time than most people deciding what to wear
- ▲ clothes are very important to you
- ▲ you are highly sexual
- ▲ you are more comfortable being "in control" of relationships
- ▲ you are easily offended
- ▲ you love parties
- ▲ you love to flirt
- ▲ you enjoy good food and wine
- ▲ you are partial to bright colors
- ▲ you love music
- ▲ you enjoy dancing
- ▲ you hate confinement on any level
- ▲ you understand logic but make the majority of your decisions based on your gut feeling

EBOS FOR OSUN More than any other single offering, Osun loves honey. She is also fond of light-colored fruits, wine, beer, rum, or gin. Hens, guinea hen, quail, and male and female goats are her blood offerings. Offerings of candies, cakes, flowers, mirrors, kola nuts, red palm oil, coconuts, and cowrie shells are also acceptable.

Osun's day is Friday.

OSUN
//////////

Osun (pronounced O-SHUN) is the personification of beauty and sexuality. As the guardian of Oshogbo, she retains, to this very day, a unique place in the pantheon of Yoruba orisa. Yoruba mythology tells how the town of Oshogbo was founded and survived due to the protection of Osun.

The settlers of Oshogbo originally lived a short distance away in the town of Ibokun. A political dispute caused many to flee and seek safety elsewhere. They were led by the previous town's crown prince and Ifa priest, Owate. They initially settled into the town at Ipole. Suddenly, as if offended, the previously abundant springs of Ipole diverted their currents into underground channels, creating a severe drought. Owate consulted Ifa, who informed him that greatness would be achieved by his descendants if they could find the river that represented all living waters, including the now-dry springs at Ipole. It was during this second pilgrimage that they came upon the river orisa Osun. Realizing that the abundant and pure waters of the river would provide them with the basis for a secure community, they decided to build their new town on the banks of the river itself.

It was then that the peaceful waters of Osun grew stormy and violent and the orisa herself rose from the river to inform the newcomers that the groves on the banks of her shores were sacred to her. If the people would build their city on the hills above the river and keep her groves sacred and unspoiled, Osun would guard and protect the city itself. The settlers agreed, and the town of Oshogbo was founded. It is interesting to note that Oshogbo, almost alone among towns and

villages, has never been conquered. During the Fulani jihad that wiped out many traditional villages, Osun appeared in the form of a camp follower, dressed only in her natural charms, and presented the soldiers with a tasty vegetable dish. This dish was highly laxative in effect, and the subsequent distress of the Fulani fighting men weakened them sufficiently to halt their progress. In this weakened state they were caught by the Ibadan armies and defeated. The city of Oshogbo had been saved. The orisa had kept her promise.

Osun, for all her beauty, sexuality, and wealth, arouses distrust in many Western women. For Osun men, who reflect her energy, the path is somewhat easier. In one sense, the very power of her movement for quintessential femininity could be seen as an impediment to the movement for women's equality. Not only is this not true, but (seriously) Osun would never give up her dominance and settle for equality! Osun is an energy force focused on the present and intimately connected and comfortable with all sensual pleasures. If you were forced to give a one-word description of the energy quality of Osun and her children, it would be *sensuous*.

Our mythology contains reference after reference to the beauty of Osun, but beauty is often culturally or societally defined. The full bodies of Goya's nudes juxtaposed to the straight lines of Twiggy give us a perfect example of how notions or standards of beauty change. Her children can be short or tall, skinny or fat, young or old, fair or dark, but they will all have a tangible sensuality that often transcends the current standard of beauty or attractiveness. Those in touch with that energy, regardless of their body style, carry themselves and behave in a manner befitting the sexiest movie stars. If you have ever been at a party where an overweight man or woman, for example, acts as if he or she were the most handsome or beautiful creature there, walks about exuding charm and the absolute confidence that you will be smitten by those charms, you have been in the presence of a child of Osun totally in touch with his or her orisa energy. That energy, that sensuality, is the core and essence of Osun and her children.

This sensuality is not a casual or hedonistic energy. It helps Osun and her children accomplish the single most important task in the life of Ifa devotees: conceiving and bearing children. The magical moment of conception is made more probable when both participants reach full sexual expression.

Osun's sensuality epitomizes the powerful, sexual female that Ifa extols. It is through this transcendent sexuality that conception can take place and our Ori called from heaven (see chapter 4) to share its next journey with the newly created fetus. In the philosophy of Ifa, children are the greatest single blessing that people can achieve. Though Osun is more than just a conceiver and deliverer of babies, it is this one aspect that places her in a position of prominence in the lives of her children and of all Ifa devotees. And though all orisa can help women who are having trouble conceiving, Osun more than any other is capable of giving children to the childless.

The sensuality of Osun also offers us an opportunity for transcendence, a chance to be open to the world of spiritual energy through orgasm. During orgasm we experience pure feeling, and afterward we are better able to cope with our routine responsibilities. That, in great measure, is what the world of spiritual energy is all about—it replenishes our energy.

It might seem that, because of her obvious and overwhelming femininity, Osun would have no male devotees. But that's not true. There are many male omo Osun. For all her abounding femininity, Osun does carry a male energy component, who is known as Ikoodi Osun. He is the messenger of the male sexual energy necessary to complete the act of conception. Male omo Osun represent the same sexual and sensual intensity in male form that daughters of Osun represent in female form. To put it simply, male Osuns are usually quite sensual and are uniquely aware of and responsive to female sensual needs and desires. The true male lover, as opposed to the performer, will likely be a child of Osun.

The sensual energy of Osun is not limited to sex or conception; this same sense of total involvement is what provides Osun's children with the road map to wealth and love. Ifa understands that money is a necessity for fully exploring and appreciating the beauty and spiritual potential of life. Rather than competing with spiritual growth, it makes it both easier and more complete. For this reason, the omo Osun who are connected to their energy should find making money easy. Keeping track of it, however, is another matter.

Osun's energy is intricate and complex. For example, in the mythology of Ifa, it is Osun who is in charge of conception and birth . . . but she may well give over her children to Yemonja to raise. It isn't that she is not, or could not be, a good mother; it is simply that her energy and talents are best expressed in a free and unfettered life-style. Osun would be a very testy orisa if she were confined to a domestic life. Similarly, her knack for making money and accumulating wealth isn't accompanied by an equal desire to take care of it. Wealth is a tool, a tool that helps us spiritually and temporally, and no one understands that better than Osun. Though perfectly capable, Osun simply won't be bothered by the mundane. It's not that she can't balance a checkbook; it's that it simply doesn't interest her.

This sense of immediacy, of absolute involvement, permeates every aspect of Osun and her children. Typical Osun godchildren could be presented with a series of totally logical arguments as to why a certain course of action should be followed, and though fully comprehending the logic of the arguments, they would invariably make their decisions based upon what they feel. This can be very frustrating to the people around them, but it is, on an energy level, the Osuns' only choice. They act on feelings.

Osun's focus on emotion often translates into oversensitivity in her children. A man who is child of Osun could have just won the lottery, received an award, or received a promotion at work, but if someone suggested that his outfit was in bad taste or he noticed a pimple or blemish on his face, his entire day would be ruined. Granted, this is a bit of an oversimplification, but Osun's tendency to take offense easily exhibits itself in many ways. With Osun herself, ridicule, disdain, or lack of respect can bring about a fury and anger that will sweep away all that stands in her way. There are no Ifa devotees, regardless of their guardian orisa, who want to incur or feel the wrath of Osun. Making it even worse is that, of all the orisa, Osun is the least likely to forgive. Once you have offended her you must go to extremes in offerings and prayers to even hope for her forgiveness. Her children have much the same trait. They are easily offended, and once genuinely injured, they will cross you off their list forever.

Osun both loves her children and provides them with the finest of everything: beautiful clothing, fine food, vintage wine, and colorful jewelry. Their love of fine things has a certain down side as well. Osun men and women must be careful not to overindulge, as extra weight or portliness is always a risk.

Osun is intimately acquainted with and adept at witchcraft. Her children have an almost instinctive ability to work freely in this area as well. Those in touch with their energy will find themselves drawn toward spells and ebos designed to strongly influence the behavior of others. With all the natural allure and sensuality of Osun, witchcraft seems almost superfluous.

Those who cannot handle flirtatious behavior had better find a mate other than an omo Osun. Though it is not imperative for Osuns to act out the flirtations, they do thrive on constant admiration and attention.

In Ifa mythology Osun was originally married to Orunmila but was attracted to and married Sango. In so doing she left Orunmila and took Sango away from his original wife, Oya. It was said Sango built her a glorious brass palace where she bore him the blessing of twins. Since that time brass has been the special metal most associated with Osun. Her children should wear brass bracelets to help connect with her energy. In the same context, children of Osun will seldom get along with children of Oya. In the visceral recesses of time, the injury and hurt felt by Sango's loyal wife Oya at losing him to Osun has not diminished or faded away. It is an undercurrent that almost invariably will strain any relationship between these two powerful orisa.

Osun's heightened sense of life creates a number of idiosyncratic traits in her children. One of the most perplexing to me is what I call the "vote syndrome." Osun's children, perhaps because of their sensitivity about how other people view them, will invariably ask a host of people their opinion about something the omo Osun is considering doing. They may ask four or five or twenty people the same question, "What do you think about . . . ?" After they have completed their poll, they will do whatever they want or feel is right regardless of the opinions the others expressed. Why then take the vote? Only Osun and her children can answer that question.

Osuns favor bright colors, music, dance, and excitement. An omo Osun, tired from the everyday workplace, will find her energy replenished by going out and having a good time. While other orisa seek peace or seclusion as a means of recharging, Osuns can play or dance into the wee hours of the night and awaken refreshed the next morning. For those living with or loving an Osun, understanding this is extremely important. If you try and fetter Osuns you will not only drain their energy, you will create a situation they will eventually leave.

In the workplace as well, Osuns need excitement or, at the very least, people contact. To place an Osun in a cubicle running a computer for forty hours a week would be the equivalent of an emotional death sentence. When Osuns do not understand this energy or attempt to exist in an inappropriate atmosphere, they become emotionally stressed and physically ill. The worlds of fashion, cosmetics, acting, photography, television, public relations, hairdressing, or modeling are environments in which omo Osun would thrive and grow.

Children of Osun will love her waters and find themselves able to fill up with her inexhaustible energy by swimming, sailing, or even soaking in a perfumed bath.

In Africa her followers wear necklaces of brass beads and favor the color yellow. The peacock is symbolic of her beauty and bearing, and five peacock feathers adorn the thrones of Osun. Mirrors and fans, along with shells and brass combs, are among the symbols that cater to and help connect her children with her. Fish are her divine messengers, and the catfish is of particular importance as an ebo or offering. It is believed that the tentacles on each side of the catfish mouth are charged with energy similar to that of the orisa. Honey, both as a symbol for sexuality and for her appetite for it, is a regular offering to Osun. Her children will often go to the water's edge and slowly pour honey into the lake or stream while asking Osun for the favor they seek.

Remember the classic tale of Osun and her sensuous dance to bring Ogun back from the forest? Osun went to the edge of the forest where she knew Ogun was living. There she began her sensuous dance. Ogun, peering out of his hiding place, watched fascinated. Osun never looked his way, but continued her rhythmic dance until nightfall. The next day she returned and continued. Each day Ogun began to creep closer and closer to this hypnotic creature. Always, Osun pretended not to see him. Finally, when Ogun had crept within arm's length, Osun reached in and dipped her fingers in the honey pot she carried on her waist. Turning quickly, she smeared the sweet substance over the lips of the startled Ogun. Tasting the honey and hypnotized by the beauty and allure of this sensual orisa, Ogun followed Osun back to civilization where growth and building could resume.

The foremost priestess is known as the Iya Osun and lives in a royal palace in Oshogbo. She is the keeper of the most sacred mystical taboos of Osun and protectress of the original sacred shrine Ojubo Oshogbo, the altar that founded the town. It is through her that Osun often appears in human form. More than any other orisa, Osun is prone to adopting human forms to communicate with or bless her followers. The tale that recounts how Osun stopped the Muslim invasion by appearing as a camp follower is an example of this.

Each year thousands of pilgrims go to her sacred groves in Oshogbo, Nigeria, and seek her blessings for children, love, and wealth. Each year many will personally experience Osun in her human aspect.

ORI

Ori ki buro ko fe de ale, ile ti iwa nikan lo soro.

No matter how bad a person's destiny may be, there is an amendment; but the more difficult to amend is an individual's character.

FIFTEEN

ORI—
AJALA MOPIN—
DESTINY

EBOS FOR ORI The most common offerings for your Ori include kola nuts, dry gin or other hot drinks, palm oil, white pigeon, and all foods. You would not use all of these at one time, but only those indicated by divination.

ORI
//////////

O ri plays an important role for Ifa devotees. The word itself, in Yoruba, has many meanings. It means head, or
the apex or highest pinnacle of achievement. In a spiritual sense, the head, as the highest point of the human
body, represents Ori. The head of a company or organization is known
as Olori, or Ori for short. The supreme being, our single God, is known
as Oludumare, another form of the word.

In the human body, Ori has two roles: the physical and the spiritual. The physical functions of Ori will be familiar to us: our brains
think, our eyes see, our noses smell, and our ears hear. Our mouths
speak and eat and breathe. Our faces are different from all others and
provide our physical identities. Our spiritual Ori are themselves sub-
divided into two elements: Apari-inu and Ori Apere. Apari-inu represents character; Ori Apere represents destiny.

An individual may come to Earth with a wonderful destiny, but if he
or she comes with bad character, the likelihood of fulfilling that destiny is severely compromised. Character is essentially unchangeable.
Destiny is more complex. In Ifa we believe that we choose our own destinies. And we do this through the auspices of the orisa Ajala Mopin,
or the god of Ori. Ajala is responsible for molding the human head,
and it is believed that the Ori we choose determines our fortunes or
tribulations in life. Ajala's domain is close to Oludumare's, and it is he
who sanctions the choices we make. These choices are documented by
what we call Aludundun deities. All of us received our destinies at this
place. An Ifa verse helps explain:

E lee mo bi olori gbe yanri O
E ba lee yan teyin
ibi kannaa la gbe yanri O
Kadara o papo ne . . .

You said had it been
you knew where Afuape
got his Ori
You could have gone there for yours.
We all got our Ori at Ajala's domain.
Only our destinies differ.

Destiny itself can actually be divided into three parts: Akunleyan, Akunlegba, and Ayanmo. *Akunleyan* is the request you make at Ajala's domain—what you would like in specific during your lifetime on Earth: the number of years you wish to spend on Earth, the kinds of success you hope to achieve, the kinds of relationships you desire. *Akunlegba* are those things given to an individual to help achieve these desires. For example, a child who wishes to die in infancy may be born during an epidemic to assure his or her departure. Both Akunleyan and Akunlegba can be altered or modified either for good or for bad, depending on circumstance. Sacrifice and ritual can help to improve unfavorable conditions that may have resulted from unforeseen evil machinations such as witchcraft, sorcery, or magic. *Ayanmo* is that part of our destiny that cannot be changed: our gender or the family we are born into, for example.

In many respects, Ori may be the most important deity in the influence of one's life. Although it would seem that everyone would choose wealth and success for their destiny, such is not the case. The reason can be found in the fact that in Ifa, material success and accomplishment, though pleasant and encouraged, are not the yardsticks of existence. That yardstick is Ori-inu, or character, and the ways of showing strong character are often not by traveling the easy path. Also, if an individual's character is bad, his or her choice of destiny may not be fulfilled. In the sacred Odu Ogbeogunda, Ifa says,

> Ise meta ni omori odo nse
> Ka fi ori re gun iyan
> ka fi idi re gun elu
> ka fi agbede-meji re ti ilekun dain-dan-in dan in
> Awon ni won difa fun
> Oriseku omo Ogun
> Won ki fun Ori liemere Omo Ija
> Won difa fun Afuwape
> Omo bibi Inu agbonmiregun
> Nijo ti won nlo ile Ajala-mopin
> Lo ree yan Ori
> Won ni ki won rubo
> Afuwape nikan lo mbe leyin to mebe
> Ori Afuwape wa sun won ja
> Won ni awon ko mo ibi olori gbe yan Ori o
> Awon ko ba lo yan ti awon
> Afuwape da won lohun wipe:
> Ibikan naa la ti gbe yan Ori o
> Kadara ko papo ni.

> A pestle performs three functions:
> It pounds yam
> It pounds indigo
> It is used as a bar lock behind the door.
> Cast divination for Oriseku, Ori-ilemere, and
> Afuwape
> When they were going to choose their destinies
> in Ajala Mopin's domain.

They were asked to perform rituals.

Only Afuwape performed the rituals.

He therefore became very successful.

The others lamented that had they known

where Afuwape chose his own Ori, they

would have gone there for their own too.

Afuwape responded that even though their

Ori were chosen in the same place, their

destinies differed.

The point here is that only Afuwape displayed good character. By respecting his faith and performing his sacrifices and rituals, he brought the potential blessings of his destiny to fruition. His friends, Oriseku and Ori-ilemere, failed to display good character by refusing to perform their rituals, and their lives suffered accordingly.

If a person's Akunleyan and Akunlegba are very bad, it can be detected on the third day after his or her birth through what we call Ikosedaya. This is a special ritual divination ceremony performed on a newborn infant by a babalawo in order to determine his or her Ori and what must be done to appease or enhance it. In the case of a bad destiny, there are only two possibilities for altering it: ritual/sacrifice and the presence of good character. Through good character individuals may be led to successful, knowledgeable people who will be prepared to guide and help them. Ritual and sacrifice can provide the same results. Using these two avenues may not make individuals with difficult destinies rich or successful, but it will certainly make their lives more comfortable.

In the sacred Odu Owonrin-Meji, Ifa says,

> Agbon mi jia-jia ma jaa [name of an Ifa babalawo] cast a divination oracle for Bayewo when she was told to perform rituals. After the rituals, she was asked to use the chameleon to rub her entire body. She complied. Shortly after, she gave birth to a baby boy. A child born after rubbing the body with chameleon is named Oga-n-rara.
>
> Oga-n-rara was coming from Heaven to Earth. He chose no single favorable destiny. When he was on Earth, life became unbearably diffi-

cult. Consequently, he approached ten different babalawos for divination. Oga-n-rara performed the rituals he was advised to perform and was able to have his needs met from Oludumare.

If our situation is honestly bad, and it is not a matter of our character or behavior, then our Ori Apere must be appeased. Prescribed sacrifices or rituals must be performed to bring ourselves back into healthy alignment. These rituals are best performed at night, and once they have been performed one is advised to stay in the house until morning. If this is impossible, then the ritual or sacrifice must be performed precisely at dawn before any other acts of the day are embarked upon.

Before performing the ritual it is essential to be freshly bathed and dressed in clean clothing. White would be the preferable color, but if dressing all in white is not possible, use the lightest colors available. Black is not acceptable. In the ritual to Ori Apere, you must wear a cap or covering for your head.

Having prepared yourself for the offering you chant three times:

Ela ro
Ela ro
Ela ro!
Ori mo pe o
Ori mo pe o
Ori mo pe o!

Orunmila, please descend
Orunmila, please descend
Orunmila, please descend!
Ori, I call on you
Ori, I call on you
Ori, I call on you!

Then you present your problem, ask for a solution, and give your offering as payment and thanks.

There are several Ifa verses that offer general prayers to your Ori
Apere. Among them are these:

Iwonran Olukun
Abara le kokooko bi ori ota
Difa fun Ore Apere
Omo atakara sola
Nje ibi ori gbe ni owo
Akara
Ori je won o ka mi mo won
Akara
Nibi ori gbe nni ire gbogbo
Akara
Ori je won o ka mi mo won
Akara.

Iwonran Olukun [Ifa babalawo]
cast divination oracle for Ori-Apere
It is certain that Apere is the quintessence
of well-being.
Wherever Ori is wealthy, let mine be included.
Wherever Ori has many children, let mine be included.
Wherever Ori has all good things of life, let mine be included.

Ori wo ibi ire
ki o gbe mi de
Ese wo ibi ire
ki o sin mi re
Ibi ope agunka ngbe mii re
Emi ko mo ibe
Difa fun Sasore
Eyi to ji ni Kutukutu owuro

Nje ti o ba tun ku ibi to dara ju eyi lo
Ori mi ma sai gbe mi de ibe.

Ori, place me in good condition.

My feet, carry me to where condition is favorable.

Where Ifa is taking me to, I never know.

Cast divination oracle for Sasore

In the prime of his life

If there is any condition better than the one I am in
at present

May my Ori not fail to place me there.

Ori mi gbe mi
Ori mi la mi
Gbemi atete niran
Gbemi atete gbeni ku foosa
Ori nii gbe ni
Ajawo, kii se oosa.

Support me, my Ori.

Make me prosperous, my Ori.

Ori is humankind's supporter before deities.

If things are going badly in your life, before pointing an accusing finger at witches, sorcerers, or your enemies, you would do well to examine your character. If you are in the habit of bullying people or not being considerate of their feelings, do not look for any real happiness in your life no matter how materially successful you may be. If, on the other hand, you help others and bring happiness to them, your life will be full not only of riches but of joy and happiness as well. But remember, it is far easier to alter your destiny than it is your character.

SIXTEEN

THE ORISA OF MEDICINE, JUSTICE, FARMING, AND FEMALE POWER

OTHER ORISA
//////////

I t would be virtually impossible to deal at any length with the entire pantheon of orisa. Those most significant and useful have been described in some detail in earlier chapters. Of the hundreds of others—including Ota, Erinmi, Jigunre, Laberinjo, Pepe, Olosa, Oranmiyan, Aje, Kori, Iroko—I have devoted this chapter to those who tend to be most significant in our everyday lives.

OSONYIN

Osonyin is the orisa of plants and the inherent *asé* and magic they contain. He, along with Esu, is the constant companion and assistant to the babalawo.

Osonyin is one-legged like the trees and plants he represents. In the myths it is said that he lost his leg and acquired other physical infirmities while in a struggle for power with Orunmila. His staff of office is forged from iron and often contains leaflike extensions topped with a single bird. The staff, known as *opa orere eleye kon,* is carried by the babalawo as indication both of his office and of his relationship with Osonyin, which allows for the transformational use of herbs. The staff, which contains a series of birds perched on the lower branches as companions to the single bird on top, is an indication that this particular path of Osonyin is obligated to the *aje,* or witches. This close association comes from Osonyin's remarkable talent for controlling the destructive powers of fear and hysteria. Through his herbal applications he can transform destructive and chaotic hysteria into creativity. Improper usage can produce the reverse effect.

The babalawo or owner of the staff must be sure it does not fall down. It must never lie on the ground, because this would break its connection with the living force, or *asé*, of plants. Plants that fall on their sides are dead and have lost their energy. Though Osonyin is bound closely to the babalawo, there is no orisa that can perform tasks without the help of this herbal orisa.

The tale is told of how Oya, discovering the secret hiding place of Osonyin's magical herbs, created a windstorm to topple their container from the immense heights of the Araba, or white silk cotton tree, that it was hidden in. This tree, the tallest in Africa, has great spiritual power and reaches heights of 120 feet or more. Osonyin heard the wind and tried to return in time, but many of the magical herbs had spilled to the ground, and all the orisa helped themselves to as many as they could before Osonyin could once again gather his treasures together.

Osonyin is owner of the forest and plants, and no other orisa can effectively use his or her magical *asé* without permission from Osonyin. He is associated with the *aje*, or witches, because he is also intimately involved with the practitioners of black magic.

Though Osonyin is intimately involved with the babalawo, priests of Osonyin perform their own ancient form of divination. The Osonyin priest joins with the magical qualities of *agemo* (chameleon). Herbal medicines are combined with *agemo*, and one half is eaten by the priest and the other half placed inside a doll. In a trance state, the priest communicates with the doll, who answers in a high-pitched, childlike voice. There is little attempt to conceal that the voice issuing from the doll is a product of ventriloquism, but the essence of the process is that the priest is communicating with energies that not only provide the questions but supply the solutions as well. The babalawo's staff, or Osun (not to be confused with the orisa of the same name), represents his pact with Osonyin to utilize the properties of herbs for magical purposes. The staff of the priest of Osonyin is similar in looks and purpose.

ORISA OKO

Oko was first man, then orisa. He was said to have been the king of Irawo. He was selected king after a highly undistinguished life that consisted mostly of roaming the land as brigand and part-time warrior. His most extraordinary talent was as a hunter, particularly of the elusive guinea hens, or bush birds, of Africa. As king, his rule was tyrannical and self-indulgent. It was this self-indulgence that touched off the events that changed his life and ultimately turned him into an orisa.

Returning from a journey, Oko found that his palace courtyard was virtually filled with wild yams from the harvest. In our tradition the yams cannot be eaten until the local priests have divined the necessary offerings and offered the requisite prayers. To partake of the yams before that takes place would be to violate a major taboo. Oko, self-centered as he was, was more consumed by his hunger from the journey than by respect for the traditional taboos of his religion. He built a large fire and proceeded to roast as many yams as he could pile upon the flames. Earth, incensed at his insensitivity, gave him the dread disease leprosy.

In ancient times lepers were offered two alternatives. They could be confined at home, without human contact, until the disease proved fatal, or they could be exiled to the wilderness; in more modern times the choice became known as "staying home" or going to the "farm." Yet, in Oko's day, the farm did not yet exist, as foodstuffs were hunted or gathered in the wild. Nevertheless, it is because of Oko's exile that the farm itself exists. When he was cast into exile in the wilderness, one of his devoted wives followed him. It was there, in their wilderness residence, that his wife began to systematically plant and harvest cultivated fields, and it was there that farming was created. In Oko's self-indulgent way, he took and was given credit for his wife's brilliance. He was credited with the creation of the farm.

Though character is a genuine issue for the Ifa devotee, pragmatic results can often override short-term judgments. Oko's belligerent attitude, his theft of the credit due his wife, and his self-absorption led in turn to his violation of taboo, illness, exile, and finally the emergence of the "farm" as a great blessing to humanity.

Today, the taboo for the newly harvested yam still exists. It lasts one lunar month. Yet, for the devotees of orisa Oko, it lasts longer. It is so strict that his followers will cover their eyes when passing piles of newly harvested yams. It is as if they must, by their acts of reverence, make up for the lack of reverence by the orisa they follow.

Finally, a month or more after harvest, when the yams are piled high at the altar of orisa Oko, and several have been offered to the ancestors, the ceremony and festival are allowed to begin. The gods eat first, humans second. Oko supervises it all.

Orisa Oko was known to hunt with an enormous sword, and today his altars reflect this. His avatars are guinea hen, poisonous snakes, and scorpions. To violate the taboo today would still bring the wrath of leprosy or death by bite or sting to the offender.

It is orisa Oko's task, in addition to farming, to search out, give trial to, and execute witches. The *aje,* or witch, is the epitome of uncontrolled forces, while the farm is the essence of controlled elements. For this reason Oko is firmly opposed to witches and spends a great deal of time eradicating them from the land. The accused are placed on the orisa throne, and priests of Oko utter the prayers known only to their cult. If guilty, the accused die. If not, they are set free.

ORISA OSOSI

Ososi is the orisa of the hunt. His primary symbols, the bow and arrow, are representative of his multifaceted capabilities. Tragically, during the kidnapping of Africans for slave trade, entire villages devoted to the worship of this orisa were uprooted and taken to the New World for sale. As a result, this once-powerful and influential African orisa hardly exists on his native continent. In the New World, in the syncretization of the religions Candomble, Santeria, Macumbe, and others, Ososi still plays a major role.

Ososi is both hunter and warrior. His ability to see great distances, hear the most minute sound, and act instantly give him the power and ability to kill with ease. He is basically a loner, traveling the woods and forests in search of game. His closest associations among the orisa would be with Ogun, orisa of iron, who also lives a solitary wilderness existence, and with Obatala, the orisa of clarity and justice. Ososi has been known to carry out the judgments of Obatala, and his own mental clarity and alertness make for a strong pairing with the orisa of purity. It is Ososi's relationship with Obatala, his carrying out of Obatala's sentences, that has led to the New World concept of Ososi as the owner of jails and prisons. Quite often, in Cuban, Brazilian, or Puerto Rican homes you will hear, "Ososi, please live in my home so I will not have to live in yours."

One of the Ososi *oriki* tells how the hunter returned to his home to find that two quail he had shot that morning had disappeared. What Ososi did not know was that his mother had visited his home and, seeing the quail, had taken them to her house to prepare them for her son. Furious at what he assumed to be thievery, Ososi instructed his arrow to find the culprit. He then shot his magical arrow into the air, and it flew to his mother's home and killed her. Later, when Ososi realized what he had done, his contrition elevated him from man to orisa, and he pledged to supply man with food from that day on. Ososi also has the capacity to use magic. His life in the forest acquainted him with herbs and their magical *asé*.

ORISA OKE

Oke is a female orisa whose earthly form is rocks and boulders. Her projections seem to defy the gravity that encumbers her fellow orisa and are most often seen jutting from the tops of hills or mountains. Even small stones and pebbles contain her *asé*, and a famous Yoruba *oriki* translates, "The smallest stone sends forth great power." Indeed, this orisa in her igneous form is the essence of power. Her natural altars, as worshiped by her devotees, often open into caves or fissures in the ground or a mountain.

Ifa devotees believe that children born in the uterine sack are Oke's chosen children. When this type of birth occurs, the sack is never cut open, but rather a single drop of sacred red palm oil is dropped upon it. It will then open without difficulty.

Animal offerings to Oke are never killed. They are brought before her natural altars and set free. It would be a great taboo to kill or capture these animal offerings, and they are assured a comfortable old age in Oke's care.

Ibadan in Nigeria is a primary center for Oke worship. The city is built on a series of hills, and one is sacred to Oke, with an altar upon it. In Ibadan, during ceremonies to the orisa, she is greeted, *"Okebadon age, olomuoro,"* which translates, "Bat's water cooler with huge breasts." Her chief priest, the Aboke, conducts her annual festival, where the Oba of Ibadan provides a cow, edible snails, beer, and yams for her devotees.

ORISA NANA BUUKUN

One of the most mysterious, powerful, and feared orisa, Nana Buukun is the mother without children. Her cult is based primarily around magic rather than mysticism. She rules prebirth femininity. Only women are her devotees. In one sense she is the witch with terrible magical powers, able to kill with a touch of her staff. In another aspect she is the protective mother, the mother of all. Her title, Iya Gbogbo, translates "Mother of Everything." The seeming contradiction—Mother of Everything, yet having no children of her own—resolves into her nannylike aspect, in which she cares for and nurtures the children and the home.

Her priestesses are adept at extrasensory feats, including teleportation. Their ability to transport themselves, instantly, from one place to another has been demonstrated time and again. The hyena is the sacred animal of Nana Buukun and reinforces her connection with the dead.

The orisa—all 401 of them—are real. They exist, not as metaphors or parables, but as genuine sources of energy contained in every aspect of our universe. The Ifa devotee or orisa worshiper is constantly striving to open his or her channels to these energies. This is not a process that can be achieved through "understanding" but only through ritual. Words and explanations can take us to the door, but if we are to enter, experience, and benefit from the vast reservoir of energy that is available to us through Ifa, words and explanations must be left outside. In many ways Ifa is the original instruction book for the rituals that allow us access to this boundless energy. Learn it, work on it, and when you are finally able to leave the words at the door and experience it, you will have found your path home.

PERSONAL OBSERVATIONS AND EXPERIENCES

Either-or may not simply confuse you . . . it may kill you.

In July of 1989, my wife, Vassa, became pregnant. For over three months she bled every day. Her health deteriorated so dramatically that we even became more concerned for her well-being than for the survival of the fetus.

In July of the following year a jury convicted a Christian Science couple of "wantonly and recklessly" causing the death of their two-and-a-half-year-old son "by relying solely on prayer" to heal the boy.

I am by birth and conditioning a Western man. I was raised to believe that science would, eventually, identify and solve all our problems. And I am a babalawo of Ifa. When my wife began to have increasing difficulty in her pregnancy, I made sure we had the finest scientific/medical help available, but I also used divination and sacrifice to help change events.

The doctors could not understand what was causing her bleeding. Finally, after a series of highly specialized blood tests, we received a call from our obstetrician, who referred us to a hematologist. It seemed that Vassa's platelet aggregation count was significantly out of the normal range. Knowing that platelets are intimately connected to blood clotting, the diagnosis made sense to me. I wondered what terrible disease might be causing it. We made an appointment with a well-known blood specialist for that Friday. On Wednesday we performed a ceremony and divination. The results were frightening. The reading strongly suggested that unless something could be done, both her life and the child's life would be in jeopardy. The ebo was to be done through Osun, the orisa of love, money, and conception, who is represented in the Yoruba pantheon by rivers and lakes.

The next day we went to the river. Vassa offered honey, a special shrimp dish that is a favorite of Osun's, and a small blood sacrifice. She also bathed and was cleansed with Osun's healing waters.

Friday we went to the hematologist. Vassa was so weak that she had to lie down across several chairs in the waiting room. This so distressed the receptionist (feeling it was not good PR for other patients to see someone sprawled ill in the waiting room) that we were moved into an examination room where she could lie down properly while awaiting the doctor. They took quite a lot of blood for testing and asked us to return the following Tuesday.

The next night we completed the call for sacrifices. Along with me, priests of Osun, Yemonja, and Obatala and a priestess of Osun worked on Vassa. For over five hours we performed major sacrifices and prayers over my wife. At 2:00 A.M.—Vassa's abdomen covered with blood, feathers, honey, and a host of other ingredients—we concluded the ritual. Her reading, performed after the ceremony, stated that all was now well. The five of us were totally exhausted from expending so much emotional energy. For the first time in months Vassa seemed more energetic, and her color had improved dramatically.

Sunday morning, for the first time in over three months, her bleeding stopped. It never resumed.

On Tuesday, we went to see the blood specialist for her results. This time Vassa, who had been improving steadily, sat alert in the waiting room. After a long wait, we were ushered into the specialist's office, and after another twenty minutes the doctor appeared. After reviewing her chart for the results of the tests, he turned to us and said, "I don't know why you're here. Your tests are perfectly normal."

At this point, I have a confession to make. My first reaction was, of course, relief. But my second reaction was typically Western. I thought, Well, the original test must have been in error. Even though the error was one that would have matched her medical problem exactly, it was still statistically possible. Then a thought flashed through my mind.

"What were the results of her liver profile?" I asked the doctor.

For over twenty years Vassa had suffered from chronic serum hepatitis. Her liver condition was monitored every six months with blood profile studies, and though it had improved over the years, it was still quite serious.

"Her liver profile is also perfectly normal," the doctor replied.

Psychiatrists would undoubtedly say that Vassa's bleeding was a product of hysteria and that the sacrifices had simply allowed all those emotions to disperse and the bleeding to end. But no matter how clinical you want to be, I can't believe that twenty years of chronic serum hepatitis could "disappear" overnight unless something very profound had occurred!

The point here is more than that we reversed a potentially disastrous medical condition; it is that we used all our alternatives to achieve our goal. We used both the linear and nonlinear that were at our disposal, the best of ritual and the best of science. In contrast to the Christian Science couple who would use only one method of healing—faith healing—Ifa understands that either-or approaches can lead to disaster. We are not, and cannot be, in a contest between faith and knowledge. We should, and must, be in a symbiotic relationship with both kinds of energy to solve our problems and improve our lives.

Ifa will never suggest that you choose between using ritual or rational skills to cure a disease, get a job, or find a mate. I teach, as Ifa has taught me, that success, growth, happiness, and health come from integrating both sides of your brain. If you're sick, see a doctor *and* use ritual help for a cure; if you're applying for a job, you might use special substances to influence the prospective employer *but also* prepare yourself for the interview and dress correctly; if you're romancing someone, you can use spiritual energy to achieve your goals, but you'd better be charming, considerate, and caring, too. And, when you get well, get the job, or get together with the mate you seek . . . don't even worry about which hemisphere won. Understand that *you* did and that it's probably because you at least doubled your effectiveness by tapping multiple sources of strength. Ifa believes in results. Let those foolish enough to be stuck in one area argue about credit.

IFA AND DRUGS

In today's culture, one of the only routes left for achieving transcendence is through drugs. Those who partake call it "getting high," I call it "reaching for transcendence," but the bottom line is that drug use is one of the very few escape routes from societal limitations and pressures that most people are aware of. I believe that this is the reason drugs are so popular. And I also believe that we will never solve the so-called drug problem until we understand this.

We all have a basic, visceral need for spiritual experience. There have always been holy places to which people could go in search of transcendence. Our churches and synagogues were established to fill this function—to give us a place in which to integrate ourselves and balance our psyches. But, with very few exceptions, they have lost their soul. They have become forums for discussions of ethics and morality. They are places to which people turn to find solutions to societal rather than spiritual problems.

I believe that our spiritual leaders have lost their way, opting to turn away from the magic and mysticism that was their *raison d'être* and surrendering their empirical truths to the rational truths of Western science. The taking of communion, for instance, was not meant to be merely symbolic; it was meant to be visceral, transcendent. Jesus said, "This is my flesh; this is my blood." The ritual of eating horseradish on Passover was intended to make us *feel* the bitterness of oppression, not simply *remind* us of our ancestors' pain. People turn to drugs because rituals like these have lost their power—the power to make lasting, positive changes in our lives.

As long as we insist on trying to "reason" people out of their thirst for transcendence, we will fail. We must recognize that it is a culture out of balance that drives people to drugs in the first place, that drug and alcohol abuse are symptoms of psyches begging for genuine highs and settling for chemical ones. Only by giving people a path to a healthy, workable, spiritual system will we render drugs unnecessary and superfluous. Ifa, through its ancient rituals—all of which have maintained their transcendent power—gives us a way to integrate the material and spiritual so that the pleasure and satisfaction we get from them both is real and long-lasting.

IFA AND CONCEPTION

It was late fall when I received a call from Nora, a client who was concerned about her best friend, who had been trying to conceive for eighteen months. Her friend had consulted specialists in the field, and after concluding there was nothing physically wrong, her doctors were about to start her on a series of hormone injections to see if she could possibly get pregnant. Nora wanted to know if there was anything Ifa could do.

Having had friends whose wives had had the same problem, and had subsequently suffered through incredible emotional peaks and valleys from what turned out to be unsuccessful courses of treatment, I urged her to bring her friend in for a reading. I explained that if Ifa couldn't help her, which we would not know until I had divined for her, she could always opt for the hormone injections later. Several weeks later, she brought Jan to see me.

Jan was thirty-one years old and had, for the last several years, managed office operations for a successful physician. Her grounding, if not her instincts, was totally linear. I remember thinking that her desire to have a child must have been terribly strong for her to have overcome what must have been skepticism to seek out the babalawo in the first place. But I also thought, "There are no accidents"; there must be a reason she was here.

Her reading was quite complex, but I could see that Osun could help her. Osun, the orisa of sweet waters, controls love as well as the act of conception and delivery. In order to solicit her help, an intricate ceremony would have to be performed. Divination had indicated which offerings and ritual we were to use. In Jan's case, obtaining Osun's help in conceiving a child would require blood sacrifice.

I remember looking at her across my desk. I knew that Jan wanted to conceive a child with her husband more than anything. I felt her fear, her increasing feelings of inadequacy, and her overpowering sadness at what she viewed as her own personal failure. I also knew that she was typically Western, and that on this, her first visit to a babalawo, I was about to suggest a course of action that might be more fear-inducing, more upsetting, more difficult to accept than the reality of her current inability to conceive. And so, as gently as I could, I began to describe the ceremony that was called for.

Jan would come in old clothes, clothes that would, like her previous inability to conceive, be thrown away after the ceremony. My daughter, a priestess of Osun, and my wife, a priestess of Obatala, would perform the ceremony under my supervision. The reason for this, quite simply, is that, despite the male ego, the act of conception and the miracle of birth are the exclusive province of female energy. The "loop" that was to be connected between Jan and Osun could best and most sensitively be accomplished by priestesses already intimately connected to, and totally comfortable with, their nonlinear powers.

After making prayers to Osun, Jan would lie on a mat where white doves and quail would be presented first to her and then to Osun. Jan would silently ask Osun to accept these offerings so that Osun would enable her to become pregnant. Jan would also thank each animal for the sacrifice it was about to make in order that her baby could be conceived. The animals would then be passed over her abdomen before being sacrificed to Osun. River water, representing the healing powers of Osun, would be rubbed into her abdomen while appropriate prayers were being said. Honey, one of Osun's favorite foods and an avatar for sex and sweetness, would be applied as well. All would be mixed with a small amount of blood from the animals and, through the prayers and energy of the sacrifice, the loop would be made.

Following this, Jan would be taken for a shower with African black soap and *omiero,* a liquid mixture of herbs sacred to the religion. She would then dress in new white clothing to reflect the "rebirth" of her spirit and physical capacity. Finally, an orange cloth she would bring would be filled with some of the ingredients of the ceremony and worn around her lower abdomen as often as possible.

I told her that if she decided she wanted to go ahead, she should let me know so that we could schedule a time and place to perform the ceremony. It took her a month to decide to go ahead, and about another month to make the preparations.

Seven weeks after the ceremony Jan called me. She had just used one of the early pregnancy tests and the results were positive! But, she said, the positive indication had been somewhat faint, and she was afraid to get too excited. I was with another client when she called, so it was several hours before I could call her back. "Jan," I said, "you should have learned from the ceremony that what we are dealing with is positive energy. And for you to 'slide back' into fear puts negative energy into your womb. Right now there is a beautiful microscopic human being forming there, and it needs all the positive energy and joy you can give it! So instead of being afraid, feel the joy, feel the happiness, feel the relief that you've managed to get what you want so badly, because when you feel it, so will your baby!"

A blood test several days later confirmed the pregnancy. Her son was born on September 21, 1991.

Iboru, Oboye, Ibosise.

Blessing asked for, blessing received.

RELEASING NEGATIVE ENERGY

In 1975, my son Adam died. One moment he was alive and well. The next moment he was gone. He was nine weeks old.

I remember receiving the terrified call from his mother. I rushed the several blocks back to our home in time to see the paramedics running out our front door carrying what looked like a rag doll in their arms. I'm now convinced that at the moment I saw my son as a rag doll rather than my beloved child I clicked into my conditioned Western frame of mind—that "ability" to see things as component parts rather than the whole that they truly are. I could "deal" with my son's death by intellectually separating it from the entirety of my life. I had succeeded at compartmentalizing.

And so, I took the devastating loss of my son and carefully placed it in one of the thousands of "file drawers" that comprise my psyche. While my response was to "get on with my life," to "put it behind me," I totally failed to even attempt to feel and to work through the grief and reach some sort of emotional equilibrium.

We think that if we can put something away where we don't have to deal with it, it will go away. And by distancing the specificity of the event from the rest of our lives, we can, as Descartes insisted, conquer the part. What Descartes and the atomists who charted the economic and emotional paths of Western society failed to see was the impact on the whole of that kind of splitting.

So we went on with our lives. We quickly sold our house and bought another so that we wouldn't have to deal with Adam's room and his memories. We became involved in a host of stimulating activities—many not in our best interests. The fact that our lives had been altered irreparably could not be changed, even if we managed to stay too busy to notice it.

Today, as a babalawo of Ifa, I see clearly that negative energy cannot be "put away." Indeed, it seems increasingly clear that as we fill our file drawers with more loss, pain, rejection, and fear, we sow the seeds of our own emotional or physical self-destruction. For, as science would agree, energy cannot be destroyed. Even if we pretend it isn't there, even if we place it in the farthest recess of the deepest drawer, it still exists. And that repressed negative energy will eventually make itself known. Down the road, we will see the results of this negative energy as they emerge in the form of cancer, heart attacks, nervous breakdowns, or high blood pressure. Doctors' waiting rooms, divorce courts, and substance abuse clinics are filled with people whose "filing cabinets" are overflowing.

As the years wore on, I "understood" that I had failed to deal with the death of my son. Believe me, I understood it . . . but I still didn't feel it.

In 1990, at age fifty, I became a father again.

Through Ifa I had learned not to be afraid of my feelings. I had learned how to feel and use in a positive manner the energy these feelings provoke. This time, rather than being angry that my wife's body was growing larger and larger, I reveled in the miracle of our child growing inside her. I helped for twenty wonderful hours as Vassa coped with the monumental process of giving birth, and I stood awestruck as the head of our son Dashiel made its entrance into the world. The pure, exquisite energy of conceiving and giving life provided me with an inner strength and joy I had never before experienced.

What does that have to do with dispersing negative energy? Well, not quite two months later, I was playing with Dashiel when suddenly a terrifying thought passed through my mind. It occurred to me that if anything were to happen to this precious infant whom I loved so dearly, I would be totally destroyed. Even the thought caused a terrible, gut-wrenching pain and constriction of my chest. But this time I didn't shove it away. I didn't file it away in a deep, dark drawer of my subconscious. Instead I sat and felt the pain, for I had learned that the pain of potential loss was equal to the love I felt for my son. To suppress the pain would diminish the love. At that moment, for the first time, I was able to feel the pain for Adam who had died fourteen years earlier.

The laserlike emotional energy of pain and loss and love gave way to tears that had waited fourteen years to be shed. As I held my newborn son to my chest, the tears for his brother ran down my face, and the positive energy of the love I had failed to express released the negative energy of loss I had refused to face. The file drawer emptied, and emotional equilibrium finally returned.

Ifa is the study and use of energy. Through a defined set of rituals and procedures, we learn first to experience, and then to use, energy to change our lives. Rather than suppressing or trying to modulate our feelings, we learn from Ifa that it is essential to feel totally. It is these feelings that ignite and allow the nonlinear side of the brain to perform its powerful functions. Ifa also understands that only positive energy can disperse or reach equilibrium with negative feelings.

FEELING OUR FEELINGS

In our society we are afraid of intense feelings. We have been taught that certain kinds of behavior are appropriate and others are not. Men and women are assigned societal roles and expectations that blunt their feelings and, eventually, blunt their ability to feel.

In the past, our emotional and spiritual lives were nourished through various rituals designed to keep the nonlinear sides of our brains open and active—communion, circumcision, the rituals of Easter or Passover or Lent, keeping kosher. But as modern religion traded its mysticism for humanism, we began to feel less and less and became more uncomfortable with profound feelings of any kind.

Ifa, the world's oldest monotheistic religion, retains its original means of transcendence. Through orisa worship, divination, and ancestor worship we keep the nonlinear side of our brains open and powerful. When we pray to our orisa or to our ancestors, we connect to powerful energy sources. When we present offerings to our orisa or to our ancestors, or when we use divination, we bridge the gap between past, present, and future in a palpable fashion. The profound energy and emotions released by these actions give us the power to improve our lives in tangible ways. They also give us the capacity to accept and experience intense feelings in our everyday lives. Feelings, like the orisa, are energy. They must be experienced to be useful. Ifa teaches us how to feel.

For years, in my role as a babalawo, I tried many methods of "reasoning" to get people to feel safe with their emotions. I asked them to pay attention to what they felt when witnessing a beautiful sunset, listening to an inspiring piece of music, or seeing a great painting. Yet I would often meet up with the argument that what I was calling "emotional" responses were actually the products of learned values. I don't really believe that, but I do recognize that people thoroughly trained in a Western model can listen to Chopin's music and not feel it, or can admire Van Gogh's technique while blocking off the pain and power that virtually leaps off his canvases. Actually, I believe that truly *linear* art would be nothing more than very complex number paintings and great *linear* music a cacophony of computer-driven tones! Nevertheless, it became clear that what I needed was an example they couldn't argue with.

I suggest that there is one moment in life when we are able to be totally tapped into the power of pure emotional energy. That is in the experience of orgasm. Indeed, if we try to get linear about it, it won't happen! Furthermore, after orgasm we feel relaxed, energized, and peaceful. I guarantee you that if we expended the same amount of energy carrying the groceries up three flights of stairs, we wouldn't feel energized, peaceful, and relaxed!

It's not simply because during orgasm we rub a nerve hard enough to cause the brain to produce endorphins. If it were that simple, heroin addicts would be the happiest people in the world! It's because for that one moment, we totally and constructively exit the linear world and enter the world of pure emotional energy and power. And that world, unlike our everyday temporal one, gives back more energy than it takes. Equally important, even though we momentarily "lose control" of the structures that we believe are totally responsible for our lives, the world does not come to an end. Indeed, after orgasm, our ability to cope with everyday events is usually stronger and more centered than before. It only makes sense that there would be other means of tapping this energy, too.

That's what Ifa is all about. It's a road map and instruction manual into the exquisite power of the nonlinear, the nonrational. Through ritual and sacrifice, orisa worship and divination, ancestor worship and prayer, Ifa provides a step-by-step guide for accessing this enormous source of power, peace, and strength.

Through Ifa, you will be able to explore ritual ways of accessing this power whenever you need it. At first you'll feel uneasy or perhaps even silly: "You mean you expect me to take a watermelon and put it in the lake while talking in my head to someone called Yemonja?!" But if, for only one or two seconds, you connect with the pure, powerful energy of the ocean that we call Yemonja, this will be your first step toward doubling or tripling your capacity to make lasting, positive changes in your life.

IFA AND THE BEAUTY MYTH

We are all trapped by a very limited concept of beauty. It is a fixation on the outward, on how things look, rather than how things are, and it's a kind of denial, a refusal to look *inside*. In that denial, we perpetuate our own feelings of helplessness and despair. New cars, new waistlines, new clothes, new partners, new hairstyles—all serve to deflect us from examining what's underneath.

Sometimes I am convinced that the orisa find us very funny. The foolishness of squeezing our feet into shoes that are too small and wearing jeans that are too tight would be so ridiculous as to preclude anger, but it would certainly encourage gales of good-hearted laughter.

For us, it is not funny at all. We truly suffer from these standards of beauty and appearance, which carry with them a denial of the death of our bodies in exchange for the guarantee of death to our souls! It is just too heavy a burden. I see so many clients who have bought into the nonsense; they're trying to find the right relationship, happiness, and personal fulfillment by changing the river's flow, by adhering to a set of values imposed by their culture.

In orisa worship there is a natural order and transition to life and the continua of death. Our Western fixation on appearances is simply an attempt to stop the flow of the river or the rotation of the earth. Not only can it not be done, it wastes our time and energy in the attempt—time and energy that could be used for growth.

I urge you not to waste that time, not to deny yourself that joy. Instead you should be laughing along with the orisa at our foolishness.

IFA AND THE NEW AGE

There is an enormous difference between valid and valuable. There are many roads to truth, but you can travel only one at a time.

We live in a fashion-conscious society. It has become increasingly fashionable in recent years to dip one's toe into the spiritual waters of ancient cultures. In the 1960s the fascination was with yoga, meditation, and the mantras of India. In the seventies and a greater part of the eighties, the trend moved west, and people sought the curative powers of the sweat lodge, the wisdom of Native Americans, oneness with nature. And the decade of the nineties is projected to be the beginning of a renaissance of interest in Africa. We can expect cowries and colorful beads to replace turquoise and silver.

All these cultures have wonderful religious insights to offer, but none can be meaningful to the spiritual dilettante! Transcendence was not designed as a cocktail party conversation enhancer. The art and artifacts of ancient cultures, expressing and reflecting their most precious beliefs, were not created to adorn the walls of fashionable homes. Without exception, the meaning of these objects and experiences was to be personal, inward, and transforming. Spiritual experiences were meant to cater to the soul, not the repartee.

Our culture, with its fixation on short-term gratification, conditions people toward a life lived on the surface. We have come to believe that only events that can be distilled into thirty-second news clips are news*worthy*. It is no wonder that we treat our religious experiences with the same attitude. The cocktail party dilettante has become the spokesperson for the religious experience. And transcendence has been denigrated from transformation to fashion.

Though there is undoubtedly something profound to be gained from any genuine spiritual journey, dabblers are predestined to miss it. They will flee just as they approach the real power and meaning of the experience. Why? Because once you have tasted the beauty, serenity, and power of the spiritual, you will be forced to rethink and reshape your values. For many, that's much too frightening. It's something you must feel and do . . . not just talk about.

There are those who will say, "There's truth in a lot of things; why shouldn't we experience them all?" The answer is practical, not philosophical. Every path has its own rules, its own truths and rituals. It is not unlike learning to fly an airplane. You learn the rules that allow you to fly safely to your destination. But if suddenly along the way you became fascinated with how helicopters fly instead and began to use those instructions to fly your plane, there's a good chance you would crash. It isn't a question of which one is right and which one wrong. It's simply that the instructions can't mix. There are many truths . . . one at a time.

So dilettantes come to Ifa and the babalawo to be fixed . . . in the short term. They want to get the girl or the guy, win the court case, increase their income, or restore their health, but they don't want to rethink the values that caused their problems in the first place. They will participate in the rituals, make the offerings, and achieve some practical results, but they will assiduously avoid the real opportunities for personal growth. When the real meaning and transcendent power of Ifa are made available to them, most cannot handle it. In some sense they have been unwittingly supported in this short-term thinking by many of the spiritual, yet practical, solutions that have been offered to them.

It is in this context that I draw the difference between something's being valid and being valuable. It is absolutely true that one can achieve transcendence with Native American sweat lodges, the practice of yoga, weekend religious retreats, t'ai chi, and so on. There are possibilities for transcendence in the Western traditions as well. Communion, Passover, Easter, bar mitzvah, or baptism are all opportunities for transcendence—but are they valuable? I would say that if the transcendent experience fails to become part of your everyday life, if it cannot go home with you, its value is lost.

As a culture we have come to accept that transcendence somehow does not apply to the everyday. We settle for the weekend experience and then accept our return to the rat race as normal.

That's where Ifa is valid *and* valuable. Ifa extols both the spiritual and the temporal. The orisa are with you always. You don't need a church or structure to access them. They are with you in the countryside and on the crowded expressway or at a business lunch. They can help you achieve peace in one and success in the other. Ifa sees you as whole and provides the ritual for keeping you that way; it cannot be understood or mastered in thirty seconds or thirty days. It is a lifelong journey without destination or goal. It is the reason trees grow and flowers bloom: not to become the biggest tree or the prettiest flower, but to express their joy at the energy of the sun, their pleasure at the nourishment of the rain and the soil. It is an integrated response to the universe of which they are a part.

Our spiritual experience is meant to be the same: a joyous response to the positive energy the universe holds out to us in abundance. It should include sharing our lives with others who love and respect us; the joy of good health; the miracle of children; the pride in accomplishment that comes from doing a job well and not harming the universe or the people living in it; and the recognition of our own godliness. We should awaken each day stimulated by the opportunity and potential it offers, not fearful and angry at what it may hold. We should be able to go through our lives fearless and secure in the knowledge that we need never be cut off from the power of our spiritual energy. We can then be sure that we're traveling a path of truth. Ifa is one such path. I invite you to join me on the journey.

Ko Si Ku
Ko Si Arun
Ko Si Eyo
Ko Si Ofo
Ko Si Akoba
Ko Si Fitibo
Ariku Babawa.

So that death is no more
Sickness is no more
Tragedy is no more
Loss is no more
Unforeseen evil is no more
Overwhelmed no more
Don't let us see the death of our father.

INDEX

ABOUT THE PHOTOGRAPHS

All of the photographs in this book were taken by Justine Cordwell, Ph.D. in 1950, while she was conducting anthropological fieldwork in various locations in what is now Nigeria. Although the film was developed, it was not until the late 1980s, at the author's encouragement, that the negatives were printed. They are being published here for the first time.